IS GOD SILENT WHEN WE HURT?

The Problem of Evil and Human Suffering:
Answers from History, Reason, and Theology

H. STUART ATKINS

WESTBOW
P R E S S®
A DIVISION OF THOMAS NELSON
& ZONDERVAN

WestBow Press books may be ordered through booksellers or by contacting:

WestBow Press
A Division of Thomas Nelson & Zondervan
1663 Liberty Drive
Bloomington, IN 47403
www.westbowpress.com
844-714-3454

ISBN: 978-1-6642-1985-4 (sc)
ISBN: 978-1-6642-1986-1 (hc)
ISBN: 978-1-6642-1987-8 (e)

Library of Congress Control Number: 2021900830

Print information available on the last page.

WestBow Press rev. date: 09/21/2021

In honor of those who suffer from Tourette's syndrome, and in loving memory of my great-grandfather, Elias C. Atkins. After tracing your incredible life from Indianapolis to Idaho and Montana, I feel like I know you. When I get through the gate, we have much to discuss.

In memory of the victims of COVID-19

All love to my wife, Pam, who as a nurse relieves the suffering of many. And to my incredible adult kids: Celeste, Keane, Gabriel, and Elaina, the parents of our first grandchild, Elisabeth Joy. And much love to my siblings: Edie, Linda, and Jonny.

I wish to thank the many individuals who have impacted my life for Christ, including those who discipled me in high school and college, the numerous professors in college and grad school, and the numerous authors I read over the years. Your numbers could fill pages. And most of all, I thank C. S. Lewis, for in my journey to Narnia, Lewis showed me the Christian faith is far more than kind, good, or just one option among many: he showed me it is true—the only option.

SOLI DEO GLORIA

CONTENTS

PREFACE

Thirty-five years after this work was originally written in 1983, we are now looking back on a vastly different world. We are amid a worldwide pandemic. At the time of this writing, nearly two million people have died worldwide from COVID-19.

Even though thirty-five years have passed since I wrote this material as a master's thesis in apologetics, over three decades has not changed the key principles and veracities in this book. True truth does not fade, migrate, or change over time, as is often falsely proposed today. New does not mean true. C. S. Lewis called it "chronological snobbery." This refers to the belief that just because a truth claim is older it is untrue. In fact, most of what passes today for modern relativistic thought is just a rehash of prior intellectual history. We've been there and done that. Few take the time to let history and critical thinking reveal that common thread, as evidenced in the current "fad" of revisionist history.

The hundreds of sources used in this book needed no revisions. I believe they hold their own and pass the test of time. My life as a digital marketing agency owner, adjunct marketing professor, dad, husband, and grandfather did not allow time for some possible updates. Judge for yourself. Forgive me if you think relevancy faded over time. I doubt it has, and I stand by my sources and conclusions.

In one sense, this book is my written testament to my walk with Christ that started on October 12, 1974. Read my personal testimony in "A Cross in an Ocean Voyage" in the appendix for what happened on that October night. Also read my letter written in 1991 to a relative and friend, Steve, who battled cancer and later succumbed to its ravages. He read this letter and book prior to his death and embraced its message. He ultimately defeated suffering and is now in the presence of Christ, forever free from pain. You are not forgotten, Steve.

Some say that religion is a "private matter," however, true truth is very much a public matter. Privacy attempts to keep truth unoffensive and controlled. Truth does not like a cage. It must come out, no matter who it faces down. Like C. S. Lewis, I found myself in "a universe with no exit" on that October night. And I've been safe ever since.

I make no apologies. As the apostle Paul stated in Romans 1:16 (NASB), "I am not ashamed of the Gospel, for it is the power of God unto salvation, for those who believe, to the Jew first and also the Greek." In short, that means all people, places, times, races, and nations. However, note that God's power to change lives is unleashed with active belief and not just ear-tickling interest. By grace, we must act and live on the power granted us for salvation. I, too, am not ashamed of the Gospel that changed my life. What follows is not a "safe dance" for safe spaces. The topic of this book is not a fit for a wet Kleenex approach. I don't have all the answers to the tough questions surrounding evil and suffering. I bow to God's infinite wisdom. In the end, I admit that on this side of eternity there are some things I just do not understand.

Currently, four world views concern me: relativism, scientific naturalism, neopaganism, and socialism. I touch on all four plus more in this book.

With relativism, there is no such thing as absolute truth. Some often say, "Truth is relative. There is no absolute truth." And yet, when hearing this statement, I often ask, "Are you absolutely sure?" To make such a pronouncement, one is caught in a self-contradictory statement. As Edward W. Younkins so aptly states: "Relativism contends that all truth is relative except for the claim that 'truth is relative.'" In addition, "What's true for you may not be true for me" is the sentiment. Well, how do they know that's true? In math, there's only one right answer to a problem, as C. S. Lewis once reminded us. The same applies to religion, especially when all the world's religions have different answers to some of the same critical questions.

With scientific naturalism, science and technology alone will solve the world's problems. This *Star Trek* dream world is just that: a dream.

Advancements in science have helped but not fully advanced humankind. We still have a problem of the heart not yet solved by science.

With neopaganism, "spirituality" has exploded, yet confusion reigns. Keep your religion to yourself, but don't make value judgments. The Judeo-Christian worldview has been discarded in a cloud of doubt. God has not spoken. He is silent, so they say. From the environment to "man-made" global warming, everything green, and back to relativism, the earth wins the day. Environmental stewardship is important. God's creation is ours to manage but not ours to worship. We attempt to "save the planet" while we lose our souls.

And fourth, despite its rampant intellectual and practical failures worldwide, democratic socialism is rising in popularity. For me, this is far more an intellectual than a "political" concern. Despite its utter twentieth and twenty-first century failures, socialism has been embraced with little or no accurate historical scrutiny. In essence, socialism is merely Marxism dressed up to go to church. It's economic makeup covering the real person. I examine the roots of socialism in chapter 2. The "free stuff" socialism offers today is a destroyer of economic growth and freedom. If Marx's thought was faulty, modern democratic socialism has caught the same virus. And yet the root of such thinking goes to the heart of each individual. Change people's hearts, and you change society. With socialism, the human condition is bypassed, thinking that government alone can solve our problems. Government has its place, but it's no panacea.

On the theological and philosophical side, attempts to reconcile the existence of God with the reality of evil often fall prey to logical fallacies or "modifications" of the nature of God. Theistic finitism "solves" the problem by limiting God; determinism reduces the relevancy of free will; dualism implies an impersonal antithesis of good and evil; universalism attempts to "sanctify" determinism in the context of eschatology; and monism proclaims evil an illusion. As we shall see, these and other "solutions" compromise truth, logic, and theology. Such attempts not only fail to solve the problem of pain and suffering, but they also turn a difficult problem into an impossible problem. Healthy confrontation with truth, rather than compromise of it, will serve the best interest of scholarship, theology, and philosophy.

However, with a blend of a biblical worldview and reason, there is practical and transcendent hope. Unlike the preceding approaches to evil and suffering, I will attempt a historical, biblical, theological, and philosophical analysis. The value of this approach is encouraged by Dr. Fredrick Copleston, who states the following concerning the problem of evil:

> There would, of course, be a great deal more to say on this subject, were one to introduce considerations drawn from theology, and any purely philosophical consideration of the problem is necessarily far less satisfactory than a treatment in which both theological and philosophical truths are utilized. The doctrines of the Fall and the Redemption, for instance, throw light on the problem of evil which cannot be shed by purely philosophical reasoning.[1]

The pages to follow will thus, with a historical and biblical foundation, attempt to synthesize the strengths of theology, philosophy, and common sense. It is hoped that this approach will bring well-rounded answers and clarifications to such an important issue.

Throughout the theological and philosophical history of the problem of evil, two schools of thought have shaped the direction of this issue: Augustinian and Irenaean. In the Augustinian system, the creature rather than the Creator is responsible for evil. Man's abuse of his free will as seen in the Fall is crucial to this school of thought. In contrast, the Irenaean school shifts the responsibility of evil toward God instead of man. Rather than an emphasis on the past, more concentration is placed on the future (eschatological in nature).

Instead of taking sides with either Augustine or Irenaeus, my approach will stress an important concept: balance. Unfortunately, the tendency is to shift to one extreme or another, rather than resting in the balance of biblical tension. Both schools of thought have their strengths and faults in relation to what scripture does and does not tell us concerning the problem of evil.

In the first four chapters, I will establish the foundation from which biblical theism approaches the problem of evil. In chapter 1, I will argue that Satan and the reality of demonic evil is not just a fairy tale. In chapter 2, part 1, I will trace man's assessment of his own human nature from classical to contemporary times. In chapter 2, part 2, I will present the biblical view of human nature. In chapter 3, the book of Job and its answers to evil will be discussed. From Job, I will then shift to the apex of biblical theism's answer to evil: Christ's redemption. Chapter 5 will, in reference to the foundation of chapters 1 through 4, utilize logic to further analyze evil and suffering. And last, chapter 6 will cover C. S. Lewis's views on pain as I discuss his two classic books: *The Problem of Pain* and *A Grief Observed*. The overriding conclusion of all six chapters is that biblical theism provides a cogent, consistent, and livable solution to the problem of evil. Biblical theism's purpose is not to supply all the answers, yet it does supply logical, acceptable, and livable answers. To demand answers to all the questions surrounding evil is absurd, merely because of humans' finite and epistemological limitations.

A subject like the problem of evil is no easy issue. I must confess that, in a topic such as pain and suffering, my understanding often outweighs my obedience. Furthermore, we must never forget that the Western culture in which we live is often drawn more toward comfort than crisis. In such a soft and technological society, we often become immune to the cold realities of evil, pain, and suffering.

There are two reasons the book that follows is not an academic exercise for me. First, with the sudden and unexpected death of my father when I was fourteen, I quickly learned the pain of grief. At that time in my life, Christ was merely a "religious figure" rather than the risen Lord that He is to me now. Had I fully known the transforming power of Christ then, such grief would have been easier to bear.

Second, since age ten, I have suffered from a rare neurological condition known as Tourette's syndrome. This condition, which to date has no cure, has given me firsthand experience regarding the realities of suffering. Although this condition is not terminal, I may face its physical and social consequences for the rest of my life. I can say with all honesty that I have learned lessons through my suffering that comfort would have never taught me. Suffering has taught me lessons in humility, patience, and trust. Suffering has also reminded me that those of us who are faced with a "thorn in the flesh" (2 Cor 12:7 NASB) also have a source outside of ourselves to which to turn for comfort. We must never forget that Christ Himself knew the reality of thorns, yet His thorns composed a crown that He chose, for the world's sake, to wear. The thorns Christ bore never hindered Him, and through His strength, they will never hinder His bride, the church.

My writing on this age-old topic is by no means groundbreaking. If anything, I've attempted to connect the dots and summarize the key questions about suffering and evil in an easy-to-read format. I've taken what many have said and organized it in a presentation for deeper understanding.

It is my sincere hope that the following chapters will both challenge the skeptic and encourage the believer.

H. Stuart Atkins, January 2021

NOTES

1. Frederick Copleston, "St. Thomas Aquinas: Creation," *A History of Philosophy*, vol. 2, part 2 (Garden City, NY: Image Books, 1962), 9.

ACKNOWLEDGMENTS

The Problem of Pain, by C. S. Lewis, copyright © C. S. Lewis Pte. Ltd. 1940. *A Grief Observed*, by C. S. Lewis copyright © C. S. Lewis Pte. Ltd. 1961. Extract reprinted by permission.

CHAPTER 1

Did the Devil Make Us Do It?

O Prince, O Chief of many throned powers, that led the embattled Seraphim to war Under thy conduct, and, in dreadful deeds Fearless, endangered Heaven's perpetual King, and put to proof his high supremacy, whether upheld by strength, or chance, or fate! Too well I see and rue the dire event That with sad overthrow and foul defeat Hath lost us Heaven, and all this mighty host In horrible destruction laid thus low, As far as gods and Heavenly essences Can perish: for the mind and spirit remains Invincible, and vigor soon returns, Though all our glory extinct, and happy state Here swallowed up in endless misery.[1]

To the detriment of modern thought, the reality of the devil has been reduced to a Halloween myth-cartoon that has little, if any, significance to contemporary life and meaning. Satan, deceptively dressed in his red devil's suit, grasping a pitchfork, and crowned with horns, generally is regarded as fiction rather than fact. But can such a portrayal be justified, particularly when we are faced with a vast array of unanswered questions regarding reasons behind the cold, stark existence of evil and suffering? Must supernatural causes and influences remain insignificant merely because the five senses cannot verify spiritual, nonhuman sources of evil? In short, Hamlet asserts this issue well as he proclaims to Horatio, "There are more things in heaven and earth, Horatio, than are dreamt of in your philosophy."[2] In this case, Satan has profoundly affected earth and must not be placed in the realm of fantasy. If Satan is fantasy, then Christ is fiction, for Christ consistently affirmed the existence of the devil.

The central contention of this chapter is as follows: a finite and created being, Satan, through the abuse of his free will, generated the reality and consequences of sin from which much of past and present evil and suffering derive their source. All too often the creation of evil is placed on God (infinite) rather than on Satan and humans (finite). Some origins of evil are thus generated by the creature, not the creator. However, this does not infer that all evil and suffering result from Satan. Indeed, there are logical and biblical reasons for utilizing Satan to answer many of the paradoxes surrounding evil and suffering.

Reasons for Satan as a Valid Starting Point for Evil

Practically speaking, the existence of evil in the world seems to many more real than the existence of God. We don't need to convince ourselves of pain, suffering, and gratuitous evil, especially considering world affairs during both the twentieth and twenty-first centuries. One knows evil is real. The question is this: Is a good and loving God compatible with such evil?

Then why use Satan as a starting point for evil?[3] Dr. Fredrick Sontag (1924–2009), the late professor of philosophy at Pomona College in California, asserts the following justification for satanic causality regarding evil:

> The virtue of beginning with the Devil is that he often is much more real to most men, and you are not burdened at the beginning of the argument with a fixed concept of God which may only have to be changed in the light of actual experience. Just as the crazy man may teach us much about sanity, so beginning with the Devil may be a better guide to God today than any positive idea of God could be.[4]

Sontag also states:

> God has done certain things (if he exists), but recently
> we have learned that there are a great number of things
> which he has not done, and such nonelections are perhaps
> more revealing of the divine intent. The arguments against
> God's existence may highlight what he has not done (e.g.,
> to create better worlds), and why, and thus illuminate his
> nature more than reasoning based upon the world he did
> create.[5]

Sontag seems to be saying two important things. First, reality is often more revealing than concept. The finite realities that man faces are often more tangible than concepts concerning divinity. However, this does not mean that concepts about God are invalid. It only means that the perceived world is more comprehensible than the world as we think it is. Because evil is so real, Satan may supply a better starting point for evil and suffering than God. Such an approach does not imply that God's attributes are of no value in an analysis of suffering and evil; rather, it helps to clarify misconceptions concerning why God allows such evil to exist.

Secondly, Sontag seems to be saying that God's silence may reveal God's sovereignty and higher purposes. Infinite "passivity" may express purpose rather than paradox. Thus, the supposed "contradictions" that exist between the problem of evil and the so-called "loving God" may in fact have hidden elements that sustain and clarify God's attributes rather than cloud them. The principalities of Satan may solve the "paradox" of God in ways few have considered.

Logically, there is a series of reasons for using Satan as a valid starting point for a finite origin of evil. First, an attempt to "reason away" God's existence is impossible to prove from a logical standpoint. For example, to assert that the existence of God can be disproved is to commit a major epistemological (the study of knowledge) blunder that assumes that finite humans can possess omniscient knowledge. No human, in comparison to the vast expanse of knowledge within and without our universe, can claim an epistemological monopoly on what is and what is not.

Dr. Alvin Plantinga states:

The theologian can therefore restate his position, maintaining that the existence of physical evil, evil which cannot be ascribed to the free actions of human beings, is inconsistent with the existence of an omniscient, omnipotent, and all-good deity. To make this claim, however, is to overlook an important part of traditional theistic belief; it is part of much traditional belief to attribute a good deal of the evil we find to Satan, or to Satan and his cohorts ... Furthermore, it is likely that any premises worth considering which yield the conclusion that hypotheses about devils are nonsensical will yield the same conclusion about the hypothesis that God exists. And if God exists is nonsensical, then presumably theism is not self-contradictory after all.[6]

Thus, if one asserts that God does not exist, this implies travels to every metaphysical and physical boundary of the universe without running into God. This shows the distinction between agnosticism and atheism. The agnostic shows honest doubt and leaves room for the possible existence of God, claiming pure atheism is intellectually indefensible. The limitations of such reasoning are self-evident, as is covered in later chapters. The Apollo space program placed man on the moon, not on God's lap.

Dr. John Warwick Montgomery asserts this exact point.

Little time should be spent on hard-boiled agnosticism, since it is tantamount to traditional atheism, and suffers from its basic fallacy; it presumes that one can (apart from any revelation of God, to be sure!) know the universe so well that one can assert the non-existence of God or the non-existence of compelling evidence for his existence. But such comprehensive knowledge of the universe would require either (a) revelation, which is excluded on principle, or (b) divine powers of observation on the part of the atheist or hard-boiled agnostic. In the latter case, atheism and the extreme agnostic position become self-defeating, since the unbeliever perforce creates a god by deifying himself.[7]

The same line of reasoning may be applied to the devil's existence. Granted, the devil is a created being, yet as with God, his existence is not open to disproof on mere assertions of his nonexistence. As with God, one cannot "prove" that Satan exists, but on the other hand, one cannot disprove it either.[8] Thus, is one left with an impasse? No, for the biblical account of Satan provides a historical, reliable, and primary source justification for the reality and influence of his existence. Furthermore, this does not mean that Satan exists because "the Bible says so," for to make such a claim is circular reasoning and assumes that the Bible is inspired by God and without error. One must thus step back and examine the evidence regarding the biblical documents. After an honest, scholarly, and in-depth study, one will soon find that the burden of proof clearly rests on the skeptic, not the Bible.[9]

The preceding leads us to specific biblical reasons for Satan as a finite starting point for evil. Regarding the Judaic perspective toward Satan, Dr. James Kallas, associate professor of theology and chairman of the division of theology and philosophy at California Lutheran College, asserts at length.

> Notice well, the Jewish discussion of the fall of the angels is not mere abstract philosophy, not merely idle speculation on the nature of the celestial scene above. He was wrestling with a problem, a deadly problem, the awesome extent of tragedy in the immediate world—and that tragedy he traced back not to God but to Satan. The exact time of Satan's fall was not an important issue. And the same thing can be said about all the other philosophical—rational questions we raise. Why did he fall? Why did God create him? These are not the essential issues. The doctrine of Satan does not even treat those issues. That is not what is important. The doctrine of Satan is not speaking to that. What, then, is the important issue?

> The very heart of the doctrine of Satan is not so much a statement about Satan as much as it is a statement about God. The one thing that the Jew is seeking to assert in his insistence on the fall of Satan is that God is not the author of tragedy! The vicious destruction of human life, the searing battering of human destiny, is not the will of God. It is the work of God's enemy. What the Jew is really saying is that he does not believe in a God who maims and cripples. He does not believe in an arbitrary capricious God who wantonly persecutes. These things are incompatible with the will of God. God is not evil. He does not cause unfair pain or undue suffering. Wherever and however suffering gets started, one thing is sure: it is not in God. It is in the enemy of God that such violence finds its bitter seed.[10]

These essential insights of Dr. Kallas distinctly express the central role of satanic reality concerning evil and suffering: God must not be prematurely indicted for the problem of evil, especially when biblical revelation establishes causal relations between Satan and theodicy. Furthermore, it is noteworthy that the Jewish perspective (Old Testament) on this issue sides with the character of God rather than confusing it. God is given the benefit of the doubt, not for sympathy, but for necessity.

In addition to the Judeo-cultural background of the biblical perspective, the Bible also solidifies both indirect and the direct connections between Satan and evil. In fact, one New Testament name for Satan (*ho poneros*, meaning "the evil one"), clearly implies evil with the very nature of Satan's character. Furthermore, numerous passages in the Gospels place Satan and evil in a direct relationship to one another. For example, in Matthew 13:36-45, Jesus explains the parable of the tares of the field. Here, a direct causal connection between evil and Satan is asserted in verse 39. Dr. E. Achilles states the following concerning this passage:

> The source of the evil is said in v. 39 to be the devil, and this prevents us giving any weakened meaning to evil (v. 38). The history of theology shows that efforts to

avoid the personifying of evil in the devil have led to a depersonalizing of God and Christ.[11]

Achilles further states:

> It should be remembered, however, that several passages in the NT trace evil to the devil. When in Matt. 9:4 Jesus accuses the scribes, and in Matt. 12:35 the pharisees, of evil thoughts, *poneros* is also to be linked with the devil. Elsewhere (Jn. 8:44) Jesus called them children of the evil. There is no neutral zone between God and the devil, where evil as something purely neutral could find its home.[12]

Hence, the biblical text is not ambiguous when it refers to Satan. Satan is not seen as a mere evil "force" who has little impact on the reality of evil; instead, he plays a central role in the stage of human events, which are plagued with the realities of suffering and evil. Indeed, Satan is central to finite suffering.

This thought is applied with additional clarity as Dr. Carl F. H. Henry writes:

> Man himself is therefore not the ultimate source or ontological ground of evil, but as the apostle John explicitly says, it is 'the old serpent ... called the Devil and Satan, the deceiver of the whole world' (Rev. 12:9; ASV, cf. 20:2). Paul the apostle likewise equates the Serpent of Eden with Satan (Rom. 16:20; cf. 2 Cor. 11:3, ASV). Man's deviant will does not fully explain the fact of evil; rather it is Satan, a living power hostile to God and external to man, who occasions human apostasy.[13]

In short, humans alone and their sinful nature does not explain the paradoxical nature of evil. And surely the reality of the material world does not supply an adequate source for evil. Therefore, Satan may in fact supply many pieces to the puzzle of theodicy. Both Satan's nature (evil) and his influence on humans and the cosmos through sin may provide more answers to questions that have heretofore gone unanswered.

The preceding mention of the biblical view of Satan is but a brief introduction of other key passages dealing with sources of evil. Further on in this analysis, the biblical explanation of evil reaches its focal point when we will examine Christ's portrayal of Satan. In addition, we have also briefly touched on the practical and logical reasons for starting with Satan relative to issues concerning theodicy. I hope this examination of the reasons behind Satan's impact on theodicy serves to justify the discussion that will follow. For it is foolish to connect or even discuss Satan's relation to theodicy unless valid reasons for doing so exist as a basis for further examination. Our task is now to analyze remaining key issues with one essential truth in mind: "An overt Devil, if properly interrogated, may be of more help here than a silent God."[14]

With the preceding foundation laid, we must now examine the existence, choice, and influence of Satan and his relation to the problem of evil. As for Satan's existence, our analysis will center on contemporary skepticism toward Satan in the fields of science and theology. Next, a discussion of free will and its application to created beings such as Satan, with specific attention placed on the abuse of Satan's will and how it affects humans and the problem of evil, will be discussed. This will then lead to the influence of Satan upon human affairs in manners which apply to theodicy. And lastly, concluding implications of this Satanic theodicy will be applied to contemporary issues in theodicy.

Satan, Science, and the Supernatural

During the so-called Enlightenment, a naturalistic seed was planted in the mind of humans that has grown into a scientific weed rather than wonder. This seed, naturalism, "is polemically defined as repudiating the view that there exists or could exist any entities or events which lie, in principle, beyond the scope of scientific explanation."[15] Thus, the natural rules out the supernatural. Anything beyond the observational reach of rationalistic science must be ruled as myth or "primitive superstition."[16]

A pointed example of this prevailing philosophy is evident in the following statement from the "Humanist Manifesto II"[17]:

We believe, however, that traditional dogmatic or authoritarian religions that place revelation, God, ritual, or creed above human needs and experience do a disservice to the human species. Any account of nature should pass the tests of scientific evidence; in our judgement, the dogmas and myths of traditional religions do not do so. Even at this late date in history, certain elementary facts based upon the critical use of scientific reason have to be restated. We find insufficient evidence for belief in the existence of a supernatural; it is either meaningless or irrelevant to the question of the survival and fulfillment of the human race. As nontheists, we begin with humans, not God, nature not deity.[18]

Although space does not allow us to deal with the logical, scientific, religious, and logical fallacies in the humanist worldview,[19] two key observations may be noted from the above. First, to say that "religion" brings nothing but problems to humankind is to confuse sociology with theology. Granted, extreme examples of extreme religious misapplication such as the crusades did not serve humanity's best interest, yet extreme examples of scientific development in atomic or chemical research have also caused havoc to humankind. Is this then to say that all religion and all science creates a disservice to humankind? Hardly, for one extreme of a religion or a branch of science does not render them all of no service, especially when both religion and science have accomplished much toward improving our world. In this case, the naturalistic humanist has turned the exception into the rule by making it absolute truth.

Second, this view believes that only nature and not "religious myths" pass the test of the scientific method. However, this assumption presupposes that theology and science do not mix. Such a view dangerously ignores the essential interrelations of theology and science, especially when one notes the methodological similarities of both the scientist and the theologian.[20]

In short, science takes precedence over the supernatural. Matters such as Satanic relations to suffering and evil are seen as mythological and mere "metaphysical" issues rather than as applicable answers to human suffering. Because Satan does not fit the naturalistic worldview, the reality of his existence seems to be fiction rather than fact. Satan fits as a "supernatural" myth, not a natural fact. Religious and supernatural contributions to contemporary problems are thus given storybook status rather than scientific credibility.

Interestingly, contemporary science has witnessed a significant rise in the reality and observation of satanic activity. Dr. Carl F. H. Henry summarizes the demonic dilemma that modern science and Western civilization faces:

> For all its horrors in the twentieth century, Western civilization has largely discredited Satan. In the forepart of the century Edward Scribner Ames wrote that "the old view of evil as proceeding from the machinations of an Evil Spirit, Satan, or the evil has nearly disappeared. That monstrous demon lives now almost wholly in profanity" (religion, p. 264). Remarkably, the very century whose intellectuals most ridiculed belief in spirits, demons and in Satan especially, has witnessed an explosion of new interest in spiritism, demonism and exorcism. In pursuing the scientific containment of the evils of mankind, even demon-possession is now declared a widely attested phenomenon and religionists have resumed the practice of exorcism.[21]

If satanic activity is declared an admitted phenomenon among the psychiatric and psychological field,[22] then why ignore theological applications of the demonic to theodicy, especially when theology provides answers to the problem of evil that scientism does not? To the service of all humankind, one must note that the object of science is, after all, to comprehend facts of the world, not to create—much less presuppose—a system into which all facts must fit willy-nilly. To look for regularities in the behavior of data is entirely legitimate, and pragmatically to expect such regularities is the quintessence of wisdom.[23]

However,

> like the naturalist, to insist that all data conform to
> ordinary expectations and fit a nonmiraculous model is
> the antithesis of the scientific spirit. Models must arise as
> constructs to fit data, not serve as beds of Procrustes to
> force data into alien categories.[24]

Satan is a reality that must be reckoned with by modern humans,
regardless of his scientific presuppositions.[25] To deny Satan's existence and
influence on mere scientific assumptions evades both science and reality.
One must not forget that the devil "is most successfully present where he
is denied, forgotten, unexpected or unnoticed."[26]

Satan and Contemporary Theology

Ironically, a similar cloud of skepticism hovers over contemporary
liberal theology. Arising to prominence around the first quarter of the
nineteenth century and based on a subjective and antihistorical framework,
liberal theology has often reduced the reality of Satan to a mere myth.[27]
Naturally, if a theological system reduces biblical events and accounts to
myth, then mythological doctrines often are the result. The myth becomes
the mandate.

For example, F. R. Tennant (1866-1957), provides a perfect case study
regarding liberal theology's view of the book of Genesis, especially when
Genesis 3 refers to Satan's influence upon the Fall of humans. Tennant
states:

> It can no longer be assumed, in the light of knowledge
> yielded by comparative mythology and prehistoric
> sciences, that the third chapter of Genesis supplies us
> with the record of a revelation of historical fact, divinely
> given at some definite time, or even with a story whose
> form and details were wholly the creation of its writer's
> inspired imagination.[28]

However, not only does Tennant's documentary criticism reflect poor scholarship,[29] but it also rests on subjectivity. Dr. Gleason L. Archer (1916-2004), former chairman of the division of Old Testament studies at Trinity Evangelical Divinity School, who holds five earned degrees, including an AB, MA, and PhD from Harvard University, asserts:

> Questions have been raised as to how seriously we are to take this whole narrative about Adam and Eve (and the serpent in the Garden of Eden) as literal history. Many prefer to regard it as a mere myth or fable (suprahistory, to use the neoorthodox term) in which the moral downfall of man is described by a fictitious episode designed to illustrate it. No decisive objections, however, have ever been raised against the historicity of Adam and Eve either on historical, scientific, or philosophical grounds. The protest has been based essentially upon subjective concepts of improbability.[30]

Ironically, in liberal theology's attempt to reduce Satan to myth, they have created their own myth. Rather than base their interpretations of Satan on objective scholarship and adherence to primary source documents, liberal theology has opted for a questionable, subjective biblical hermeneutic rather than allowing the text to speak for itself. Furthermore, liberal theology's "dismissal of all this Satan talk as sheer mythology is just as disconcerting as the modern brushing aside of theology in general, for as part and parcel of the biblical system of theology and ethics the doctrine of Satan appears in a spiritual context that expressly repudiates mythology and false gods."[31] To lower Satan to a mere myth is, in essence, an attempt to place humans themselves, not scripture, as the authoritative standard by which truth is to be judged. Satan as myth is the negligence of subjective scholarship rather than the verdict of an objective, historically reliable Bible.

The thinking of one of the most influential theologians of the twentieth century, Karl Barth,[32] also reflects a denial of Satan's existence. Although Barth opposed the evolutionary optimism of Darwin that saw man as inherently good, he still, like scientism, ignored key supernatural elements regarding Satan. In fact, Barth, during his lecture series at the University of Chicago Divinity School (April 23-27, 1962), directly denied the reality of Satan's existence.[33] Dr. John Warwick Montgomery, who attended the Barth lectures while a faculty member at the University of Chicago, gives the following account of E. J. Carnell's questions to Barth regarding Satan during one of the discussion sessions:

> Carnell questioned Barth's refusal to assert the ontological existence of the devil, and quoted Billy Sunday's well-known comment: "For two reasons I Believe the devil exists: first, because the Bible says so, and second, because I've done business with him." Barth countered by saying (and this drew applause—especially from the Divinity School contingent) that the attitude of Jesus and the Gospel writers to the existence of the devil is not to be considered sufficient reason for our affirming it.[34]

Because Barth was one of the most influential theologians of his day, the ramifications of his opinions were widespread in the theological community. As scripture was "becoming" the word of God, Satan was becoming the myth of humans. Along with the growth of neoorthodox, liberal theology came the denial of satanic realities as exemplified in Barth's Chicago lectures. Liberal theology thus chose to "stay abreast of the times" rather than adhere to an inerrant, authoritative, and objective scripture. Hence, Satan was rationalized and not realized.

Concerning Barth's view of Satan, the late Gustaf Wingren, a Swedish theologian, writes:

> There is in Barth's theology no active power of sin, no tyrannical, demonic power that subjects man to slavery and which God destroys in his work of redemption. There is no devil in Barth's theology. This is a constant feature in his theological production.[35]

With Satan thus left in a subjective and mythological-fable category, liberal theology has been tried and found wanting.[36] Our task is now to turn from theological skepticism to biblical affirmation.

Satan and the Old Testament

From the skeptical realm, we must now move to biblical affirmation regarding Satan's existence and influence. Unlike certain aspects of contemporary science and liberal theology, both the Old and New Testaments clearly uphold the existence of Satan. From the range of the primary source documents of the New Testament, including eyewitness and apostolic accounts, and the life and teachings of Christ and the apostles, Satan is real and active.

The Old Testament does not consistently portray the activities of Satan. Satan is present yet not predominant. Thus, "the full picture of Satan's evil character is not given in the few OT references to him, but clearly the recorded glimpses of his activities reveal that he acts in opposition to the best interests of men."[37] Furthermore, in the Old Testament (Septuagint [LXX]), the term for Satan occurs twenty-one times, with 75 percent of these occurring in Job 1 and 2. Literally, the Greek word for Satan (*diabolos*) means adversary or wicked opponent.[38] In addition, rather than concentrate on controversial passages, we must analyze the clear passages. Our purpose here is to affirm the definite passages, not interpret the controversial ones. Three Old Testament passages stand out as the strongest affirmation of Satan's existence and nature: Job 1, Zechariah 3:1, and 1 Chronicles 21:1. While other Old Testament passages also refer to Satan in a figurative manner (Ezekiel 28), we will concentrate on the most direct and literal passages.

In Job 1:1-6, one notes four significant observations: First, Satan was momentarily in God's presence. Second, Satan and God are in direct communication with one another. Third, Satan had been covering the geographic territory of earth. And fourth, God grants Satan permission to afflict but not kill Job.

From these brief observations, one must note that God speaks to beings, not myths. Clearly, Satan executes his realm of influence on earth, thus carrying his evil tactics out in the human sphere. However, despite his global influence, Satan can only affect men to the degree that God allows him.

A second Old Testament passage that refers to Satan is 1 Chronicles 21:1 (NASB), which states: "Then Satan stood up against Israel and moved David to number Israel." In this passage, Satan presents himself both volitionally and mentally to David. David gave in to Satan with the result of sinful guilt, God's displeasure, and God's judgment upon Israel. Both the mention of Satan's influence on David and the judgment of God for David's disobedience were clear indicators of Satan's tactics and power. To oppose the historical channel of God's salvation, Israel, was in essence an attempt to destroy the only valid cure for theodicy, namely, redemption through Messiah.

The last significant Old Testament passage on Satan is Zechariah 3:1-2 (NASB), which asserts:

> Then he showed me Joshua the high priest standing before the angel of the Lord, and Satan standing at his right hand to accuse him. And the Lord said to Satan, "The Lord rebuke you, Satan! Indeed, the Lord who has chosen Jerusalem rebuke you! Is this not a brand plucked from the fire?"

In this passage, God shows Zechariah a vision of Joshua before the angel of the Lord. Again, Satan is seen as accusing both humans and the works of God. Yet Satan's accusations are quickly thwarted as God renounces the devil's attempt at falsification. Indeed, Satan is not an equal nor a match for the infinite, personal God of Abraham, Isaac, and Jacob. Again, specific reference is given to Satan's name, tactics, and influence.

Satan and the New Testament

In contrast to the Old Testament, the New Testament presents a more comprehensive and descriptive analysis of the person and works of Satan. The following list of names provides an excellent summation of the New Testament view of Satan:

He is called "Abaddon" and "Apollyon" (Rev 9:11, NASB), both meaning "the destroyer"; "the accuser of the brethren" (Rev 12:10, NASB); "the adversary" (*antidikos*, 1 Pet 5:8, NASB); "Beelzebul" (Matt 12:24, NASB); "Belial" (Beliar, 2 Cor 6:15, NASB); "the deceiver of the whole world" (Rev 12:9, NASB); "the great dragon" (Rev 12:9, NASB); "an enemy" (Matt 13:28, 39, NASB); "the evil one" (Matt 13:19 38, NASB); "the father of lies" (John 8:44, NASB); "the God of this world" (2 Cor 4:4, NASB); "a liar" (John 8:44, NAS*B*); "a murderer" (John 8:44, NAS*B*); "the prince of the power of the air" (Eph 2:2, NAS*B*); "the ruler of this world" (John 12:31; 14:30; 16:11, NAS*B*); "the ancient serpent" (Rev 12:9, NAS*B*); "the tempter" (Matt 4:3; 1 Thess 3:5, NAS*B*).[39]

Clearly such attributes are the description of a being whose character parallels much of the evil and suffering in the world. Indeed, could a creature with the above nature and power be ruled out as a significant influence toward evil and suffering? Hardly—Snow White and Satan do not mix.

Moreover, since Christ represents the central purpose, goal, and figure in the New Testament, his view of Satan is essential. No other figure, because of His claim to deity (which is supported by fulfilled prophecy, miracles, His resurrection, and His own claims), is in the position to speak more authoritatively on the person of Satan. Furthermore, the central purpose of Christ's ministry was the overthrow and defeat of Satan. Dr. Henry states:

> From his resistance to Satanic temptation in the wilderness through the commissioning of disciples whose task included the exorcising of demons in his name, Jesus portrays Messiah's work as the reversal and defeat of Satan's malevolence. If Jesus perpetuated a religious tradition that he knew to be false, how could he be exonerated from the charge of deception, especially since he depicted his entire mission to the redemptive overthrow of Satan?[40]

In fact, Christ not only gave verbal assent to Satan's existence and works, but Jesus had a direct, verbal, empirical, time-space, personal confrontation with Satan himself, as recorded in Matthew, Mark, and Luke's gospels.

For example, in Matthew 4 one notes a meeting of the diabolic and deity. The Lord Jesus Christ and Satan are together in the ring of spiritual conflict, which reveals four observations about Satan. First, Christ and Satan meet in a geographical location, the wilderness. In other words, this was not just some "confrontation in the clouds" but instead the spiritual placed in the empirical. Second, Satan came to Christ, not the converse. For, as is often the case (e.g., the Garden of Eden and Job), Satan is never passive but instead often starts evil inertia. Evil and suffering do not just "appear," for their effects can often be traced to an actual cause. Third, Christ emphatically addresses Satan twice, from which we noted earlier that God does not speak to "myths." And fourth, the extent of Satan's reign was obvious when he showed Christ "all the kingdoms of the world, and their glory."[41] "Jesus did not dispute Satan's claim to sovereignty over this world,"[42] thus Christ was well aware of the extent and power of Satan's influence.

Besides Matthew's attestation of Satan's existence, nature, and confrontation with Christ, the Gospel of Luke also reveals Jesus's temptation. The significance of this account lies in Luke's reputation as one of the most accurate historians in history.[43] Such accounts of Satan's activities are well documented in New Testament manuscripts, which, when placed under the scrutiny of history, reliability, and scholarship, stand the test of authenticity.[44]

As an excellent summation to the essential value of the scriptural accounts of Satan, Dr. Vialliam Pitch, BD, MA, and PhD from the University of Glasgow, asserts:

> To avoid a doctrine of Satanology is to dodge the reality of human responsibility and deny human hope, since moral evil is then understood as one of the inevitabilities of finite existence. This the Scriptures never do. They see evil against the background of a mighty, invisible, demonic spirit world—but a world which can be resisted

and overcome through grace. The temptation of our Lord in the wilderness is understood as a contest with the devil and the whole biblical evidence leads only to one conclusion, namely, that God sent His Son into the world to combat and overthrow Satan.[45]

Satan's Choice: An Abuse of Free Will

Progressing from the reality of Satan's existence, *we* must now examine the central ramification of this existence to evil and suffering: Satan's fall. Satan's existence alone has little impact unless revelation exists that substantiates that Satan did indeed fall, thus abusing his God-given free will. This in turn offers a possible explanation for the arrival of sin.

Regarding such a rebellion, Christ Himself does verify a satanic fall account. In Luke 10:18 (NASB), Jesus states that He "was watching Satan fall from heaven like lighting." Additional parallel passages such as 2 Peter 2:4, Revelation 12:7, and Jude 6 also speak of the same incident. But how does Satan's fall relate to theodicy? It relates exactly to the area of free will and its application to suffering and evil. Because Satan was a created being, he possessed a free will, which he in turn abused.

C. S. Lewis comments on this exact issue:

> Let us not forget that Our Lord, on one occasion, attributes human disease not to God's wrath, not to nature, but quite explicitly to Satan [Luke 13:16].[46]

Lewis discusses an essential element of Satan's relation to theodicy, namely, the abuse of free will. Subsequently, our purpose will not rest in a defense of free will but instead an explanation of free will through definition and example.

At its root, free will is the volitional choice one makes without the restraint of outside wills or restrictions. In short, it is the faculty of individual choice irrespective of the results or consequences of those choices. Free will is the compass of decision regarding any choice one makes if that decision is independent of any outside influence. Or, as Webster defines free will: "freedom of decision or of choice between alternatives ... the freedom of the will to choose a course of action without external coercion but in accordance with the ideals or moral outlook of the individual."[47] Consequently, with respect to Satan (and humankind), the choice made by his will (i.e., to disobey God), carried moral consequences of great magnitude.

Dr. Alvin Plantinga summarizes this issue as he applies free will to created beings:

> Now God can create free creatures, but He can't cause or determine them to do only what is right freely. To create creatures capable of moral good, therefore, He must create creatures capable of moral evil. and He can't give these creatures the freedom to perform evil and at the same time prevent them from doing so. As it turned out, sadly enough, some of the free creatures God created went wrong in the exercise of their freedom; this is the source of moral evil. The fact that free creatures sometimes go wrong, however, counts neither against God's omnipotence nor against His goodness; for He could have forestalled the occurrence of moral evil only by removing the possibility of moral good.[48]

In the preceding quotation, Satan fits well under the category of "free creatures." God granted both Satan and humans free will so they could exist as creatures, not robots. Yet the consequence of the abuse of their wills started the inertia of moral evil. Evil is far more than just the absence of good—it is the presence of disobedience.

God is often blamed for allowing evil, yet such an accusation fails to consider the implications of free will. For example, if an innocent father's twenty-year-old son is convicted of first-degree murder, who is to blame, the father or the son? Granted, the son was cared for and strongly influenced by his father over the years, yet this does not make the actions of two separate individuals identical. The son possesses an entirely separate will from that of his father, thus he alone is responsible for his moral actions. To think otherwise would place any judicial system on the road to an infinite regression of casual chaos.

In the same manner, God is not responsible for the actions of His creatures if they possess free will.[49] Finite, human free will nullifies an infinite and "inconsistent" standstill. Satan, through the abuse of his free will, is thus a plausible starting point for sin's entrance into the arena of evil. This choice in turn initiated the beginning of much of the evil and suffering in the human realm.

As a closing thought to the preceding issue, the late Dr. D. E. Hiebert, professor of Greek and New Testament at Mennonite Brethren Biblical Seminary, reminds us:

> With Satan's substitution of his own will for that of his Maker there began the protracted conflict between good and evil which has extended through the ages. God has permitted the effort of Satan to establish his own will in opposition to the divine will to be thoroughly tested. The unrelenting conflict between the kingdom of God and the kingdom of evil is the direct result of Satan's determination to establish his claim. The presence of sin, suffering, and death reveal the inevitable consequences of the Satanic claim.[50]

Conclusion

Thus far, we have attempted to justify and analyze the existence and reality of Satan in light of both skepticism and affirmation. Satan's fall in relation to free will then followed with an explanation and example of this fall to evil and suffering. On logical, scientific, theological, and biblical grounds, an attempt has been made to erase the fallacies surrounding the existence and influence of Satan on the problem of evil. Clearly, the burden of proof lies with the skeptics. Until Satanic applications to theodicy can be proved otherwise, is it not safe to travel the course of the preceding analysis?

Yet what practical and theoretical applications to theodicy does Satan indeed show us? May the following five guidelines act as a means of transferring the realm of Satan to the realm of Seriousness.

First, Satanic applications to theodicy shift the blame of evil and suffering to the creature rather than the creator. God's love and omnipotence are not the problem; Satan and humans are.

Second, Satan is a logical source of evil. Evil is conceived in the womb of finite existence, not infinite "inconsistencies" concerning the attributes of God.

Third, evil is inconsistent with a perfect and holy God, yet consistent with fallen creatures. A God who sent His Son to die for sin does not create such sin.

Fourth, the distinction between finite causation and infinite permission must be made. Fallen creatures are one of the many factors pertaining to the reason for evil and suffering, but not because God caused the evil. God permitted evil out of love in order that He would not violate the free will of His creatures.

And fifth, the reality of sin and its results as initiated through Satan answers many questions regarding theodicy. One's view on the nature of humans, for example, has vast implications on the problem of evil, especially when Satan was instrumental in wounding human nature.

Perhaps the epistle of Paul to the Ephesians best proclaims the relation of Satanic realities to the problem of evil:

> For our struggle is not against flesh and blood, but against
> the rulers, against the powers, against the world forces of
> this darkness, against the spiritual forces of wickedness in
> the heavenly places.[51]

The cast in the theater of God's creation is not limited to Satan alone. Act 2 introduces yet another creature in whose existence and nature there is no question: humankind. Satan is not the sole criminal regarding evil—humans are also to blame. Our task now is to shift to anthropology.

NOTES

1   John Milton, *Paradise Lost*, ed. Robert Vaughn (London: Cassel, Petter, and
     Galpin, 1866), Book 1, Lines 127-41.

2   William Shakespeare, *Hamlet*, Act I. Scene V, ed. E. K. Chambers (Boston: D.
     C. Heath, 1893), 48.

3   This is not to suggest a subjective ontology as a sound starting point for
     theological propositions. Scriptural revelation, which supplies the
     epistemological justification of Satan's existence, and not "being assertions," is
     the foundational basis behind such an approach.

4   Fredrick Sontag, The *God of Evil: An Argument from the Existence of the Devil*
     (New York: Harper, 1970), 4.

5   *Ibid.*, 5.

6   Alvin Plantinga, *God and Other Minds* (Ithica, NY: Cornell University Press,
     1967), 149-51.

7   John Warwick Montgomery, *The Suicide of Christian Theology* (Minneapolis,
     MN: Bethany Fellowship, 1970), 254-55.

8   The logician Irving M. Copi makes a crucial point concerning the proof of
     being and nonbeing as applied to legal reasoning. This is significant, especially
     because Christ's claims to deity, by the tests of legal evidence, can be supported
     "beyond a reasonable doubt."[See Simon Greenleaf, "The Testimony of the
     Evangelists," *The Law Above the Law* (Minneapolis, MN: Bethany House,
     1975), 91-140.] Thus, Jesus's assertions of the existence of Satan may also be
     accepted on the same grounds. Copi writes: "The fallacy of *argumentum ad
     ignorantiam* is illustrated by the argument that there must be ghosts because
     no one has ever been able to prove that there aren't any. The *argumentum ad
     ignorantiam* is committed whenever it is argued that a proposition is true
     simply on the basis that it has not been proved false, or that it is false because
     it has not been proved true. But our ignorance of how to prove or disprove a
     proposition clearly does not establish either the truth or the falsehood of that
     proposition. This fallacy often arises in connection with such matters as psychic
     phenomena, telepathy, and the like, where there is no clear-cut evidence either
     for or against. It is curious how many of the most enlightened people are prone
     to this fallacy, as witness the many students of science who affirm the falsehood
     of spiritualist and telepathic claims simply on the grounds that their truth has
     not been established. Although this mode of argument is fallacious in most
     contexts, it should be pointed out that there is one special context in which it
     is not fallacious—namely, in a court of law; for in a court of law the guiding
     principle is that a person is presumed innocent until proved guilty. The defense

can legitimately claim that if the prosecution has not proved guilt, this warrants a verdict of not guilty. Since this claim is based upon the special legal principle mentioned, however, it is quite consistent with the fact that the *argumentum ad ignorantiam* is a fallacy in all other contexts." [Irving M. Copi, *Introduction to Logic* (New York; Macmillan, 1982), 101-2.]

9   See the following works: B. B. Warfield, *The Inspiration and Authority of the Bible* (Phillipsburg, NJ: Presbyterian and Reformed Publishing, 1948.); Norman L. Geisler, *Inerrancy* (Grand Rapids, MI: Zondervan, 1979); John Warwick Montgomery ed., *God's Inerrant Word: An International Symposium on the Trustworthiness Of Scripture* (Minneapolis, MN, : Bethany House, 1974); Gleason Archer, *Encyclopedia of Bible Difficulties* (Grand Rapids, MI: Zondervan, 1982); John W. Haley, *Alleged Discrepancies of the Bible* (Grand Rapids, MI: Baker Book House, 1981); F. F. Bruce, *The New Testament Documents: Are They Reliable?* (Downers Grove, IL: InterVarsity Press, 1982.)

10   James Kallas, *The Real Satan: From Biblical Times to the Present* (Minneapolis, MN: Augsburg Publishing, 1975), 41-44.

11   E. Achilles, "Evil, Bad, Wickedness," *The New International Dictionary of New Testament Theology*, vol. 1, ed. Colin Brown (Grand Rapids, MI: Zondervan, 1979), 566.

12   *Ibid.*, 567.

13   Carl F. H. Henry, *God, Revelation, and Authority*, 6 vols. (Waco, TX: Word Books, 1976-83), 6: 244-45.

14   Sontag, *op. cit.*, 13.

15   Arthur C. Danto, "Naturalism," *The Encyclopedia of Philosophy*, vol. 5, ed. Paul Edwards (New York: Macmillan, 1967), 448.

16   See Robert E. D. Clark, *The Universe: Plan or Accident?* (Philadelphia: Muhlenburg, 1961), 219-36.

17   The "Humanist Manifesto," first drafted in 1933, and signed by a number of intelligentsia, represents the basic "doctrinal statement" of the Humanist movement. Interestingly, the optimistic view of human nature that this document initially held to was quickly changed after World War II. The document is strongly naturalistic, humanistic, and optimistic toward truth and man.

18   "Humanist Manifesto I and II," (Buffalo, NY: Prometheus, 1976), 16.

19   See Norman Geisler, *Is Man the Measure?* (Grand Rapids, MI: Baker Book, 1983), 111-83.

20   See John W. Montgomery, "The Theologian's Craft: A Discussion of Theory Formation and Theory Testing in Theology," *The Suicide of Christian Theology* (Minneapolis, MN: Bethany Fellowship, 1975), 267-313.

21   Henry, *op. cit.*, 249-50.

22　In 1975, Jan. 8-11, under the auspices of the Christian Medical Association, a symposium was conducted at Notre Dame University on the topic of demon possession. Doctors, psychiatrists, anthropologists, theologians, and psychologists attended to present papers and discuss this issue. For a collection of the papers presented, see the following work. In addition, for a clinical admission of the reality of demon possession, see the page numbers noted in the same work: John Warwick Montgomery ed., *Demon Possession: A Medical, Historical, Anthropological, and Theological Symposium* (Minneapolis, MN: Bethany House, 1976), 223-68.

23　John Warwick Montgomery, *Faith Founded on Fact* (Nashville: Thomas Nelson, 1978), 69.

24　*Ibid.*, 70.

25　See: A. E. Wilder Smith, *Man's Origin, Man's Destiny* (Wheaton, IL: Harold Shaw, 1969.); Carl F. H. Henry ed. *Horizons of Science* (New York: Harper and Row, 1977); Anthony Standen, *Science Is a Sacred Cow* (New York: E. P. Dutton, 1950).

26　Henry, *op. cit.*, 250.

27　Carl F. H. Henry, *Christian Personal Ethics* (Grand Rapids, MI: Baker Book, 1977), 175.

28　F. R. Tennant, *The Sources of the Doctrines of the Fall and Original Sin* (Cambridge. MA: At the University Press, 1903), 1.

29　For a superb analysis of the shortcomings and limitations of documentary and form criticism, see C. S. Lewis, "Modern Theology and Biblical Criticism," *Christian Reflections*, ed. Walter Hooper (Grand Rapids, MI: William B. Eerdmans, 1982), 152-66.

30　Gleason L. Archer, *A Survey of Old Testament Introduction*, (Chicago: Moody, 1979), 200-201.

31　Henry, *op. cit.*, 237.

32　Barth's view of evil sheds additional light on his theology. Basically, Barth defined evil as "nothingness." He writes: "And this is evil in the Christian sense, namely, what is alien and adverse to grace, and therefore without it. In this sense nothingness is really privation, the attempt to defraud God of his honor and right and at the same time to rob the creature of its salvation and right. For it is God's honor and right to be gracious, and this is what nothingness contests. It is also the salvation and right of the creature to receive and live by the grace of God, and this is what it disturbs and obstructs." [Karl Barth, *Church Dogmatics: The Doctrine of Creation*, 3. 2, eds. G. W. Bromiley and T. F. Torrance (Edinburgh: T. and T. Clark, 1960), p. 143, cited in Vernon R. Mallow, *The Demonic: An Examination into the Theology of Edwin Lewis, Karl Barth, and Paul Tillich*, (Lanham MD: University Press of America, 1983), 50.]

33 The tapes of this lecture series are obtainable at the dean's office of the University of Chicago Divinity School. They are not sold to the public.

34 John W. Montgomery, "The Theologian as Reporter: Barth in Chicago," *The Suicide of Christian Theology* (Minneapolis, MN: Bethany Fellowship, 1975), 192.

35 Gustaf Wingren, *Theology in Conflict*, trans. Eric H. Wahlstrom (Philadelphia: Muhlenberg, 1958), 25.

36 See J. G. Machen, *Christianity and Liberalism* (Grand Rapids, MI: Eerdmans, 1923).

37 D. E. Hiebert, "Satan," *The Zondervan Pictorial Encyclopedia of the Bible*, vol. 5, ed. Merrill C. Tenney (Grand Rapids, MI: Zondervan, 1978), 282.

38 H. Bietenhard, "Satan, Beelzebul, Devil, Exorcism," *The New International Dictionary of New Testament Theology*, vol. 3, ed. Colin Brown (Grand Rapids, MI: Zondervan, 1979) 468.

39 D. E. Hiebert, *op. cit.*, 282.

40 Henry, *op. cit.*, 238.

41 Matt. 4:8

42 D. E. Hiebert, *op. cit.*, 283.

43 F. F. Bruce, *The New Testament Documents; Are They Reliable* (Downers Grove, IL: InterVarsity, 1982), 90-93.

44 *Ibid.*

45 Fitch, *op. cit.*, p. 54, 55.

46 C. S. Lewis, *The Problem of Pain* (New York: Macmillan, 1962), 133-36.

47 *Webster's New World Dictionary of the American Language* (New York: World Publishing, 1970) 557.

48 Alvin C. Plantinga, *God, Freedom, and Evil* (Grand Rapids, MI: Eerdmans, 1980), 30.

49 See Edward John Carnell, *An Introduction to Christian Apologetics* (Grand Rapids, MI: Eerdmans, 1948), 303.

50 D. E. Hiebert, *op. cit.*, 284.

51 Eph. 6:12 (NASB).

CHAPTER 2

Anthropology and Evil: A Historical Survey (Part 1)

Part 1

I go on and on, and I don't know where I'll find myself next—in stench and disgrace or in light and joy. And that's where the main trouble lies: everything in this world is a puzzle. Whenever I've sunk into the deepest shame of depravity—and that has happened to me more often than anything else—I've always recited that poem about the goddess Ceres and man's fate. But has it reformed me? No.[1]

Twenty-first century humanity is surrounded by vast and outward achievements in science, medicine, and technology, yet an essential facet of human nature remains to be accurately assessed: the *inner* man. All too often the outward success of man has led to his inward bankruptcy. Humankind progresses toward a superficial utopia until human wickedness exposes its potential in events such as World Wars I and II, 9/11, and other actions of human depravity. Mankind is then briefly corrected and humbled, yet soon seems to head in the direction of another round of utopian games and hopes.

Ironically, social, economic, and technological progress has seemingly done little to improve and supply inward, lasting correctives as to why humans are capable of generating much of the suffering and evil in our contemporary world. Humankind's power to change and alter his or her surroundings has never been greater. Yet the vast examples of human suffering and evil have not decreased despite this technological progress.

Throughout the history of humankind, attempts at explaining human nature are often plagued with inconsistent and unrealistic applications. Although there is generally value in such attempts, only biblical theism, grounded in the historic Christian faith, provides a balanced, realistic, and accurate appraisal of humanity's nature, especially as it relates to the problem of evil. Once human nature is accurately assessed, many questions regarding evil and its source are answered. In short, human nature supplies the sinful nature of evil and suffering.

In our study of human nature, our analysis will take us in two directions. First, in part 1, a historical look at humans from the classical, Patristic, Medieval, Renaissance, Reformation, Enlightenment, and Modern periods will be attempted. This brief historical sweep is not intended to give the "final analysis" on all human history, but its main service is to provide a general overview and critique of humanity's view of himself or herself throughout the centuries. Second, this historical survey will serve as an effective backdrop and foundation from which to contrast biblical Christianity's view of human nature. Within the view of the biblical theist, in part 2, the Old Testament, New Testament, Pauline, and Christological perspectives of humanity will be considered.

Human Nature and the Classical Period

From the depths of classical thinking, as characterized in Plato, Aristotle, Stoicism, and Epicureanism, comes one of the oldest and most significant worldviews pertaining to man's interpretation of himself. Overall, classical thinkers regarded man as distinct from nature in the possession of his rational faculties. In classical thought, reason reigned. Plato's view of the logos, forms, and "the Good" and Aristotle's emphasis upon man as "a rational animal" are clear examples of such a rationalistic mind-set. Plato, in *Meno*, asserts through Socrates:

> If then virtue is something in the soul and it must be
> beneficial, it must be knowledge, since all the qualities of

the soul are in themselves neither beneficial nor harmful, but accompanied by wisdom or folly they become harmful or beneficial. This argument shows that virtue, being beneficial, must be a kind of wisdom.[2]

The late Dr. Fredrick Copleston, professor of the history of philosophy at the University of London, whose sixteen-volume work, *A History of Philosophy*, is considered by many the standard in its field, states the following about the status of "reason" in the thinking of Plato:

Plato's ethic is eudemonistic, in the sense that it is directed towards the attainment of man's highest good, in the possession of which true happiness consists. This highest good of man may be said to be the true development of man's personality as a rational and moral being, the right cultivation of his soul, the general harmonious well-being of life.[3]

Thus, for Plato, knowledge and reason act as a form of intellectual salvation. Since man's intellectual faculties are his highest treasures, reason must shape the evaluation, essence, and virtue of human nature. Human nature is thus a "reasonable" nature. In addition, Plato's stress on reason is evident in his view that education is essential for a good society. Reason, when channeled through education, thus produces a virtuous society.[4]

Aristotle, in his *Nicomachean Ethics*, states:

Wisdom and prudence—this, the virtue of one part of the intellect, that, of the other—are of necessity desirable in themselves, even if neither of them produces any concrete result. Yet a result they do produce. Wisdom produces happiness, not as the doctor's art produces health—where the doctor or his art is the efficient cause—but as a healthy state if the body produces it. For wisdom is part of virtue as a whole, thus making its possessor happy by its exercise if not by its mere possession.[5]

H. STUART ATKINS

Concerning Aristotle's view on reason, Copleston states:

> Now, if happiness is an activity and an activity of man, we
> must see what activity is peculiar to man. It cannot be the
> activity of growth or reproduction, not yet of sensation,
> since these are shared by other beings below man: it must
> be the activity of that which is peculiar to man among
> natural beings, namely, the activity of reason or activity
> in accordance with reason. This is indeed an activity of
> virtue—for Aristotle distinguished, besides the moral
> virtues, the intellectual virtues.[6]

Again, one notes a parallel between Plato and Aristotle: reason is the virtuous quality in man. Because Aristotle stressed the reasoning faculties of man, he too held that the mind is the master of virtue and purpose. The classical period may indeed be characterized as a period where reason was seen as not just a mental expression but instead a moral attribute. Hence, for the classical mind, man is "enslaved only by the irrational. The free man thus achieves his freedom through the apprehension of the rational good."[7]

Critique of the Classical Period

Although the stress on reason in the classical period was not without value, reason does not always imply rightness. For example, Hitler's Germany was characterized by one of the most educated societies in history, yet did reason reduce the unjust evil of the concentration camps? Furthermore, if education, as Plato declared, was essential to virtue, then why is crime so prominent in our contemporary, knowledge-based, online world? Virtue is not a necessary result of reason and education. Education produces knowledge, not a guaranteed morality.

In addition, Plato's idea of the philosopher king as the most efficient ruler also includes key weaknesses. The question must be asked, "If only the wise must rule, then who will rule the wise?" What standard, besides subjective "wisdom," will determine what is best for the needs of all citizens? In fact, Plato himself realized the fallacies of such thinking when he was invited to Syracuse to educate Dionysius II and failed. Dionysius was a terrible leader. Plato then wrote *The Laws*, where he states in 7:15, "The Laws must be the ruler over the Rulers." Hence, "unrestrained power to the wise elite must be severely criticized."[8] An attempt at using reason as the source of human virtue deals with the symptom and not the cause of irrational and immoral actions. Reason itself is an inadequate answer to a lack of human virtue.

If ignorance and irrationality are the cause of evil, then knowledge and reason must solve the problem of evil. But such thinking not only begs the question; it also ignores the presence of evil in both rational and educated societies and men. Reason does not solve the problem of evil. At best, reason can speculate, but it cannot eradicate the problem of evil. Analysis alone is not adequate when tangible solutions are needed.

The Patristic Period

In the period of the church fathers, influences from the classical and Hellenistic eras were strong. During this period, man's view of anthropology changed, a shift which carried vast implications for the past and the present. For example, in Irenaeus, Tertullian, and Origen, anthropology became more analytic in approach. Irenaeus separated the "higher" and "lower" segments of the soul. Tertullian proclaimed the essential corporeality of the soul and defined the *Imago Deo* as man's imperishability. And Origen sided with Plato on the preexistence of the soul (a view which was later condemned), in addition to teaching a dualism toward the flesh.[9]

As for the nature of man, there existed two motifs of thought during the patristic period: the Pelagian and Augustinian. In Pelagian thought (Eastern church), Adam's fall was the first of a progression of sinful acts.[10] In the Augustinian system (Western church), Adam's fall was a corrupting influence. Man is thus guilty and depraved toward performing good.[11]

Although Pelagianism is plagued with vast logical and theological problems,[12] "Augustine is the brightest star in the constellation of the church fathers, and diffuses his light through the darkest periods of the middle ages, and among Catholics and Protestants alike, even to this day."[13] Even though Augustine's thinking was not without problems (i.e.,

Neoplatonism), his anthropology was more realistic and balanced than that of the classical period.

To summarize Augustine, we must look at his central motifs of thought. Augustine's view of man divides into three stages: the innocent state (*status integritatis*), the corrupt state (*status corruptionls*), and the redemptive state (*status Redemtionis*).[14] Augustine asserts in his basic anthropology:

> God, the Author of all natures but not of their defects, created man good; but man, corrupt by choice and condemned by justice, has produced a progeny that is both corrupt and condemned. For, we all existed in that one man, since, taken together, we were the one man who fell into sin through the woman who was made out of him before sin existed. Although the specific form by which each of us was to live was not yet created and assigned, our nature was already present in the seed from which we were to spring. And because this nature has been soiled by sin and doomed to death and justly condemned, no man was to be born of man in any other condition. Thus, from a bad use of free choice, a sequence of misfortunes conducts the whole human race, excepting those redeemed by the grace of God, from the original canker in its root to the devastation of a second and endless death.[15]

Critique of the Patristic Period

From Augustine's words above, it is obvious that he left no room, apart from redemption, for man to restore himself by his own means. Because all men are born depraved, sin has a causal connection to the problem of evil. In his acceptance of scripture's teaching, and because of his own personal battle with depravity (i.e., his wild life in Carthage as a young man, which produced an illegitimate son), Augustine was aware of the realities of human wickedness. In addition, he was also aware of and appropriated the Christian hope of salvation in Christ, which resulted in such works as *The Confessions* and *The City of God*. Augustine relied on biblical revelation to determine the causes of evil and suffering.

Unlike some of the other church fathers, Augustine seemed to predominately derive his anthropology from scripture rather than philosophic influences. This is not to say he was without philosophic presuppositions, for there are Platonic elements in his thinking.[16] For Augustine, sin was central to anthropology:

> To sum up the Augustinian doctrine of sin: This fearful power is universal; it rules the species, as well as individuals; it has its seat in the moral character of the will, reaches thence to the particular actions, and from them reacts again upon the will; and it subjects every man, without exception, to the punitive justice of God. Yet the corruption is not so great as to alter the substance of man, and make him incapable of redemption.[17]

The anthropology of the patristic period was generally characterized by a realism toward human nature. Except for occasional heresies, human nature was seen as God's image mirrored in man. Although this image was marred through the abuse of free will, man was still capable of restoration by way of the cross. Such an anthropology is favorable because of its realism to the actual human condition. It matches reality with a solid foundation in biblical Christianity.

The Medieval Period

From an anthropological perspective, the early medieval period inherited the Augustinian system. Yet, a synthesis of Augustine and Pelagius resulted in semi-Pelagianism. This synthesis is characterized by men such as Abelard, who emphasized freedom and separated the motive from the act (Pelagius).[18] In contrast, Anselm believed "original sin was negative and privative, rather than aggressive and positive" (Augustine).[19]

Subsequently, Thomas Aquinas, the greatest theologian of the Middle Ages, expounded a blend of both Aristotle and Augustine. As Dr. Schaff writes, works-righteousness was the core in Aquinas's system:

> Penance is efficacious to the removing of guilt incurred after baptism. Indulgences have efficacy for the dead as well as the living. Their [Augustine and Aquinas] dispensation belongs primarily to the pope, as the head of the Church. The fund of merit is the product chiefly of the super abounding merit of Christ, but also the supererogatory works of the saints.[20]

Aquinas utilized the thinking of both Aristotle and Augustine. Copleston writes:

> It must be emphasized that though St. Thomas adopted Aristotelianism as an instrument for the expression of his system, he was no blind worshipper of the Philosopher, who discarded Augustine in favor of the pagan thinker.[21]

With the preceding background in mind, note the following as Aquinas explains his basic anthropology:

> Man's nature may be looked at in two ways: first, in its integrity, as it was in our first parent before sin; secondly, as it is corrupted in us after the sin of our first parent. Now in both states human nature needs the help of God, as First Mover, to do or will any good whatsoever, as was stated above. But in the state of integrity of nature, as regards the sufficiency of operative power, man by his natural endowments could will and do the good proportioned to his nature, which is the good of acquired virtue; but he could not do the good that exceeded his nature, which is the good of infused virtue. But in the state of corrupted nature, man falls short even of what he can do by his nature, so that he is unable to fulfill all of it by his own natural powers, let because human nature; is not altogether corrupted by sin, namely, as to be shorn of every good of nature, even in the state of corrupted nature it can, by virtue of its natural endowments, perform some particular

good, such as to build dwellings, plant vineyards, and the like; yet it cannot do all the good natural to it, so as to fall short in nothing. In the same way, a sick man can of himself make some movements, yet he cannot be perfectly moved with the movement of one in health, unless by the help of medicine he be cured.

Hence in the state of the integrity of nature, man needs a gratuitous strength superadded to natural strength for one reason, viz., in order to do and will supernatural good; but in the state of corrupted nature he needs it for two reasons, viz., in order to be healed and, furthermore, in order to carry out works of supernatural virtue, which are meritorious. Beyond this, in both states man needs the divine help that he may be moved to act well.[22]

Aquinas's anthropology can thus be summarized in three points. First, man's nature is seen in its prefall state of integrity. Man still needs God in such a condition, yet more for added moral strength than for redemption. Second, the postfall human nature has no hope without divine redemption. In addition, such a state can still accomplish good through a merit-type of activity. Third, God's grace is the foundation of human virtue, irrespective of a prefall or postfall condition.

Critique of the Medieval Period

To best evaluate the medieval period, one essential factor must be stressed in light of contemporary, secular society. To the medieval, the existence of God was an accepted premise, rather than a debated presupposition. Whether a medieval scholar was a philosopher or theologian, "it may be as well to admit from the very start that, owing to the common background of the Christian faith, the world presented itself for interpretation to the medieval thinker more or less in a common light."[23] Medieval anthropology was overall a biblical anthropology with seeds of classical and Augustinian thought. Because God's existence was not questioned, man's view of himself was shaped by his theological framework. In addition, "Medieval civilization had been society-oriented, not individual-directed (the feudal, manorial, gild, and ecclesiastical systems fitted men into predetermined community patterns), and the established character of society had given to all activities a timeless quality and a lack of concern for sources."[24]

Furthermore, even though Aquinas held to the reality of man's fall, his optimistic view of human nature is problematic. It is at this juncture that Aquinas represents a definite break from the Augustinian system:

> Generally speaking, the Dominicans, following the lead of Thomas Aquinas (c. 1224-1274), attempted to assimilate Aristotle by adopting a framework within which divine grace was seen as completing and fulfilling human nature, rather than dramatically abrogating it in the Augustinian manner. Consequently, the Thomistic tradition represented a separation, at least in principle, of philosophy from theology and a more optimistic view of human nature, society, and the civil state.[25]

Although Aquinas's contributions to anthropology were significant, his confidence in human nature left open a subtle, semi-Pelagian optimism which tended to nullify and weaken the safeguard of the Augustinian view of human nature. Where, one must ask, should the line be drawn between "goodness" and depravity? The equation of depravity + goodness + merit + grace seems to sink in a sea of contradictions. Hence, like the patristic period, the medieval viewpoint, as characterized by Aquinas, is favorable because of its transcendent reference point. Despite the period's optimism toward human nature, its anthropology was seen in light of man's most vital essence: the *imago deo*.

The Renaissance Period

One of the richest and most profound periods of human history is the Renaissance. Never had so much culture, knowledge, art, and creativity been synthesized and expressed. Phillip Schaff provides a fine summary of the Renaissance:

The intelligence of Italy, and indeed of Western Europe as a whole, had grown weary of the monastic ideal of life, and the one-sided purpose of the scholastic systems to exalt heavenly concerns by ignoring or degrading things terrestrial. The Renaissance insisted upon the rights of the life that now is, and dignified the total sphere for which man's intellect and his aesthetic and social tastes by nature fit him. It sought to give just recognition to man as the proprietor of the earth. It substituted the enlightened observer for the monk; the citizen for the contemplative recluse. It honored human sympathies more that conventual visions and dexterous theological dialectics. It substituted observation for metaphysics. It held forth the achievements of history. It called man to admire his own creations, the masterpieces of classical literature and the monuments of art. It bade him explore the works of nature and delight himself in their excellency.[26]

Although the Renaissance was marked by a resurgence and return to Greco-Roman literary and cultural sources, a new breed of individual was also born. Leonardo da Vinci, Michael Angelo, Dante, Brunelleschi, and many more were men who shaped the intellectual and creative landscape during this period.

Probably one of best examples of Renaissance anthropology was Giacomo Zabarella (1552-89), who believed that man's soul "was a function of the body, and that reason was the principle of natural life in the body. While man was finite, yet he was immortal in the sense that intellect does not perish."[27] In addition, Gioranni Pico (1465-94) upheld the dignity of man and believed that man is unique, not because he is God's creation, but because man possesses freedom. Pietro Pomponazzi (1462-1525) developed a restatement of Aristotle's view of the soul and its immaterial and immortal nature.[28]

Overall, the humanists of the Renaissance emphasized the dignity and competence of man. Such humanism, however, should not be equated with contemporary humanism. Renaissance humanism represented a *restauratioliterarum* of the classic humanities, not a retreat to "secular humanism."

Philosophically, Platonism was the dominant motif of the Renaissance mind.

> The dominant philosophical viewpoint of the Renaissance was a revived Platonism—or, to be more precise, a representation of the views of Neo-Platonists such as Plotinus, who had intensified the mystical side of Plato's teachings. For the Platonic idealist, the idea or the ideal is never fully represented in the objects of our experience, so satisfaction with what we have can never be complete.[29]

But Aristotelianism was by no means ignored in this period. In many of the Renaissance thinkers, Aristotelianism was evident in philosophical terms like *proposition*, *entitas*, *realis*, materia, *forma*, and *essentia*. In fact, during the close of the Renaissance, works were produced to show that Plato and Aristotle were in basic agreement, except for words and nonessentials.[30] It is thus safe to say that in many respects the Renaissance view of man is an echo of Plato and Aristotle.

Critique of the Renaissance Period

Considering the preceding summary of the Renaissance, such a period must be seen with great respect and admiration. By bringing man to intellectual and cultural heights never before reached, the Renaissance revealed an essential truth regarding man: the cultural and intellectual depth of such accomplishments places man's origin, nature, and potential in a divine light. This is not to say man is a god; it is to say he is gifted by God.

Although the Renaissance operated in an androcentric rather than a theocentric framework, biblical theism was an essential source of Renaissance thought:

> The Renaissance of the 15th and 16th centuries, whose strength was drawn from biblical antiquity, whose greatest

artists, philosophers, explorers, and litterateurs were consciously operating with a Classical-Christian world-view, and whose weaknesses and excesses relate directly to the hubris and anti-Christian Prometheanism of some of its lesser representatives.[31]

The arrogance and confidence of some aspects of Renaissance thinking was a significant weakness during this period. Man was often seen as the standard or "measure of all things." For example, Giovanni Pico della Mirandola writes in his essay *The Dignity of Man* that God placed man in the focal point of the universe and then decreed the following:

> We have made you neither heavenly nor earthly, neither mortal nor immortal, so that, more freely and more honorably the molder and maker of yourself, you may fashion yourself in whatever form you shall prefer. To man it has been granted to have what he chooses, to be what he wills.[32]

During the Renaissance, it was this arrogance that ignited danger signals. This is not to say that man has no dignity or significance in his world; instead, it is to say that realism and balance rather than arrogance should guide man's view of himself. Furthermore, Renaissance man was faced with a difficult tension between "medieval religiosity" and "medieval corporateness" on one hand, and "modern individualism" and "modern secularism" on the other.[33] The theology of Thomas was at odds with the discoveries of Da Vinci. Theology and Renaissance rebirth met in a transitional period from the sacred to the secular, yet with an attempt to retain both. With the Reformation ahead, both the secular and the sacred of the Renaissance were yet to have its full impact on future history and anthropology.

The Reformation Period

If the momentum of the Renaissance had not been slowed and influenced by the impact of Reformation thinking, a radical difference in the contemporary view of man may have resulted. Of the Reformation, Schaff writes:

> The Reformation was a republication of primitive Christianity, and the inauguration of modern Christianity. This makes it, next to the Apostolic age, the most important and interesting portion of church history.[34]

Regarding the transition from the Renaissance to the Reformation, Schaff goes on to state:

> The Protestant Reformation assumed the helm of the liberal tendencies and movements of the renaissance, directed them into the channel of Christian Life, and saved the world from a disastrous revolution … it built up new institutions in the place of those which it pulled down; and for this reason and to this extent it has succeeded.[35]

Led by Martin Luther (1483-1546) in Germany and John Calvin (1509-64) in Switzerland, the Reformation "boldly proclaimed the Bible as its sole source of authority and truth. With the church's insistence on salvation by grace and works rather than by grace through faith in the finished work of Christ (justification by faith), a radical, theological movement exploded out of the works of Luther and Calvin. From this reaction against the established ecclesiastical structures, three fundamental principles surfaced which characterized the Reformation mind: First, the supremacy of the scriptures over tradition. Secondly, the supremacy of faith over works. And thirdly, the supremacy of Christian people over an exclusive priesthood."[36]

As for Luther's view of man's nature, we read:

> Who could be so foolish as to say that man's natural powers are still uncorrupt when we know (by experience) that they are lost? The uncorrupt natural powers were (true) knowledge of God, faith, love, reverence (for God), and the like. These powers the Devil so corrupted by the Fall that man no longer loves God, but avoids Him. Indeed,

he is at enmity against Him and would rather live without God (than with Him). Here, then, there is described the corruption which took the place of man's original righteousness and honor. For, what greater disgrace could there be than the perversion of the will, the corruption of the mind, and the total depravity of reason! Does all this mean that man's natural powers are still uncorrupt? Let us therefore flee this error as the greatest perversion of Holy Scripture. Because of our innate corruption, there (now) are in our nature ignorance of God, (carnal) security, unbelief, hatred against God, disobedience, impatience and other grievous perversions which are deeply implanted in our nature. And this whole (corruption) man seeks to cover.[37]

Thus, for Luther, man's fallen nature is characterized by total avoidance of God. In addition, the wicked nature of man is obvious in man's actions and rationalizations regarding sin. The Fall is no superficial matter but instead represents a deep wound on man's nature. Man is fallen, and only through justification by faith in Christ can God restore our true nature.

Calvin's basic anthropology is characterized by a fourfold division of man. Calvin writes:

Let us examine what kind of righteousness is possible to man through the whole course of his life; let us, indeed, make a fourfold classification of it. For men are either (1) endowed with no knowledge of god and immersed in idolatry, or (2) initiated into the sacraments, yet by impurity of life denying God in their actions while they confess him with their lips, they belong to Christ only in name; or (3) they are hypocrites who conceal with empty pretenses their wickedness of heart, or (4) regenerated by God's Spirit, they make true holiness their concern.[38]

Like Luther, Calvin saw man as fallen and alienated from God. Man either attempts relief from his fallen nature in "truth substitutes"

41

or he clings to the cross for forgiveness. Christ alone is the key for the anthropologies of Calvin and Luther.

Critique of the Reformation Period

In short, the Reformation represented a return to a theocentric anthropology. The only hope for man was salvation in Christ. Neither man nor the "church" was to dictate his origin, nature, and destiny. Instead the scriptures supplied the reference point that was to mirror an accurate view of man and his relationship to his Creator. Man was to be God's creature and servant, not his own deity. Justification through faith in Christ was foundational to Reformation anthropology.

As John Warwick Montgomery asserts concerning a summary of Reformation thinking:

> Ideologically, the Reformation concerned itself with the individual in the presence of God. For Luther and for Calvin it was inconceivable that a man could stand before God except as a result of God's own gracious acceptance of the man; no longer would participation in the communal religious life of the medieval church be accepted as a substitute for a personal relationship with God based on His own gift in Jesus Christ. Salvation thus came to be described in Biblical terms rather than ecclesiastical terms, in personal terms rather than in collective terms, and in theocentric terms rather than anthropocentric terms.[39]

Hence, the Reformation, though not without faults, supplied significant contributions toward an objective view of human nature. Based on the redemption of Christ, man could turn to an anthropological absolute for gauging human nature. Furthermore, the most potent solution to the problem of evil—redemption in Christ—was praised as the cornerstone of Reformation thinking. God's Word, God's Son, and God's grace were the salvation of both the soul and mind of a wayward mankind.

Following the Reformation, one century remained before man's thought shifted toward a post-Christian age. This transitional period, known as the era of classical Protestant orthodoxy, represented the last stronghold of biblical theism before the secularism of the Enlightenment. Montgomery writes:

> The 17th century systematized the insights of the Reformation and endeavored to apply them consistently to all areas of experience. The Puritans were thus active participants in the last great epoch of integrated Christian thought just prior to the onset of the modern secular era. Because of their biblical orthodoxy, the Puritan fathers had an uncompromising anthropology: they held, as the Bible does, to man's total depravity. For them man was utterly incapable of saving himself; in the words of Scripture, "every imagination of the thoughts of his heart was only evil continually."[40]

In light of this historical shift, one must note "that the most fundamental 'break' in the history of Western civilization came at the time when the great heritage of Classical and Christian ideas lost its place as the central focus of Western life, and was replaced by a fundamentally different approach to life characterized by depersonalization and materialism."[41] Hence, the emergence of modern secularism found its origin after the classical Christian era. With the rise of the Age of Reason during the eighteenth century, a series of new anthropologies surfaced. Our task is now to turn to the Modern Period of the eighteenth and nineteenth centuries.

The Modern Period and the Age of Reason

In general, the rationalistic thinkers of the eighteenth century placed their interests "in philosophical speculation, mathematical calculation, and scientific experimentation."[42] In addition, naturalism and rationalism reached their prominence with men such as Newton, Locke, Berkeley, Hume, Reid, Rousseau, Condillac, Diderot, D' Holbach, Voltaire, Leibniz, Wolff, Lessing, and Kant.

The thinking of these men was in direct opposition to the biblical theism of orthodox Christianity. Dr. Crane Brinton, McLean Professor of Ancient and Modern History at Harvard University, writes:

> First, in this extreme form Enlightenment is a repudiation, and in some respects an antithesis, of much of Christian belief. Enlightened denial of any kind of transcendence of the external world, of personal immortality, of the whole fabric of Christian sacraments, and enlightened reflection of the dogma of original sin, as well as much more in the Enlightenment, is quite incompatible with orthodox Christianity, Catholic and Protestant alike. In fact, most of our own contemporary world views which reject Christianity for some form of secularist faith— positivism, materialism (notably Marxism), rationalism, humanism, "ethical culture," and the rest—have their origin in the Enlightenment.[43]

The Enlightenment thus represented the most significant change in the thinking of Western man since the incarnation. The reference point of a transcendent God was replaced with the admiration of naturalistic scientism and man's rational faculties. Such a radical shift in thinking spread directly to man's perception of himself. With "sin" erased from reality in the name of metaphysics, man now embarked on a path that has led to the hopelessness and fallacious worldviews of the nineteenth century. With this in mind, we must now turn to a brief analysis of post-Enlightenment anthropology.

Nineteenth Century Anthropology: Post-Enlightenment Results

Because the Enlightenment denied the relevancy of biblical theism to man, numerous presuppositions and schools of thought surfaced to replace the "truths of the past." With man's thinking now divorced from a transcendent reference point, several worldviews surfaced. Each has had a profound influence on contemporary life and meaning. We will examine the following five thinkers who generally portray nineteenth-century anthropology: Karl Marx, Sigmund Freud, Jean-Paul Sartre, B. E. Skinner, and Konrad Lorenz. These five thinkers will provide the final analysis on our historical survey of how man views himself.

Marx: Man as a Social Creature

In a visit to the reading room and first floor exhibits of the British museum in London, one quickly notes the impact of Marx's thinking on contemporary society. On seeing Marx's original manuscripts, letters, and documents, one notes that present-day communism found its conception in these beginning writings and documents of Marx.

At the root of Marx's social philosophy lies a human philosophy of who man is; in short, Marx viewed man as consisting of a *social nature*.[44] Marx himself stated that "the real nature of man is the totality of social relations."[45] It is not the inward nature of man that shaped his nature, but rather the outward, socioeconomic environment that formed human personality. Hence, to improve man, one must improve the social environment. The outside cleanses the inside.

Not only did Marx attribute "sin" to improper socioeconomic conditions, but he also denied the reality of life after death.[46] Consequently, Marx's thought was permeated with a naturalistic and materialistic view of history that ruled out any supernatural influence on the history of man. As Dr. Leslie Stevenson, lecturer in logic and metaphysics at the University of St. Andrews, observes:

> By inverting Hegel's view as Feuerbach had suggested, Marx came to see the driving force of historical change as not spiritual but material in character. Not in men's ideas, and certainly not in any sort of national or cosmic personality, but in the economic conditions of men's life, lay the key to all history. Alienation is neither metaphysical nor religious, but really social and economic.[47]

H. STUART ATKINS

Critique of Marx's Anthropology

The greatest fallacy of Marx's anthropology lies in his view of human nature, namely, that socioeconomic conditions and not man himself are the cause of "evil." Marx argues from general to specific rather than from specific to general. He seems to think that economics came before man rather than man before economics. Since man created the initial socioeconomic conditions, an attempt to change these conditions leads simply to a chaotic circle. In short, Marx attempts to solve a human cause with a socioeconomic symptom. Montgomery asserts:

> Ironically, however, Marxism here falls into the lamentable error of Western "social gospel" liberalism (Walter Rauschenbusch, *et al.*) as well as of the very "utopian socialism" which Engels dismissed as an "infantile disorder": the error of believing that man's difficulties are no more than the product of external social conditions; change those conditions, we are told, and man's problems will evaporate.[48]

Furthermore, Marx's naturalistic attempt to rule out religious truth as valid represents serious problems. Marx's presuppositions toward religious truth were bathed in a naturalistic/materialistic framework, which saw religion as "the opiate of the people." Such a framework rules out religious truth despite the logical fallacies inherent within such naturalistic reasoning. This style of "theological negativism" is more a product of the climate of opinion surrounding Marx's milieu than the result of sound scholarship and logic. In fact, Jacques Ellul, former professor of the history and sociology of institutions in the Faculty of Law and Economic Studies of the University of Bordeaux, who is a Christian with sympathies and high respect for Marx, strongly disagrees with Marx's theological conclusions.[49]

An essential question must now be asked: Just what solution does a socioeconomic interpretation of anthropology provide to solve the problem of evil? Considering the preceding material, the answer is clear: none. One must arrive at this conclusion because of the plethora of evidence that exists in the socioeconomic worlds of both the East and West.[50]

In the West, human technological potential seems limitless, yet has technology eliminated crime, divorce, war, and injustice? As for the East, in parts where industrialization and technology have influenced society (e.g., the Soviet Union), ethical violations (e.g., human rights) and social injustice are constant reminders of human wickedness. Indeed, where is the classless society of which Marx spoke? One must not forget that since the Marxist revolution in Russia, between fifty-five and sixty-three million people have died innocent deaths—hardly an adequate figure to support a socioeconomic solution to evil. Clearly, the solution to the problem of evil is far deeper than the ideological and political doctrines of nations, be they East or West. Human evil is no respecter of capitalism or communism.

Ironically, both communism and biblical theism possess similar yet incompatible doctrines.

> The truth is that Christianity and communism are antagonists that resemble each other. Private property is to communism what Original Sin is to Christianity. Communism demands faith that, with the elimination of private property, an age of perfect peace, prosperity and freedom will follow. Indeed, communism promises no less than a return to the Garden of Eden—but with no forbidden fruit![51]

It is precisely "the Eden of Communism without forbidden fruit" that renders it an unworthy and inaccurate anthropology. To deny sin leaves one of four options: (1) rationalization of internal, human wickedness, which leads to superficial solutions through "social means"; (2) the creation of a relative morality that allows the ends to justify the means, thus "defining" away sin and ethical absolutes; (3) total antinomianism, which leads to societal chaos and eventual elimination of law, order, and society; and (4) a "Christianity without tears" attempt at a utopian society (e.g., Huxley's, *Brave New World*).

Although the preceding four options are similar and interrelated, this analysis must tell us one thing: a true solution to human evil must pierce the heart of humans, not merely their environment. Improving the human environment does not improve the inner human—it merely improves the surroundings in which he or she lives.

Freud: Psychoanalysis and Human Nature

From socioeconomic conceptions, we now shift to the psychoanalytic conception of man as characterized in Sigmund Freud (1856-1939). Freud, Moravian born and trained as a physiologist in Austria, treated all phenomena on a "scientific basis," including human nature.[52] To summarize both Freud's theological and scientific viewpoint, Dr. Stevenson writes:

> He [Freud] made no theological assumptions (he was in fact a convinced atheist), not any metaphysical assumptions like Plato on the Forms, or Marx on the movement of history. What he did assume (no doubt from his training in nineteenth-century science and his research in Brucke's Physiological laboratory) is that all phenomena are determined by the laws of physics and chemistry, and that even man himself is a product of natural evolution, ultimately subject to the same laws.[53]

Freud's thinking centers around four divisions of human nature: determinism, unconscious mental states, drives or instincts, and developmental stages.

From a deterministic standpoint, Freud believes that every event can be traced to a mental cause. For example, slips of the tongue, faulty actions, and dreams have their conception somewhere in the mind. In short, hidden and secret mental causes surface in symptoms, which indicate certain problems or distortions.[54]

Second, Freud stressed unconscious mental states as a cause of certain aspects of human behavior. Unconscious desires linger in the mind, which cause seemingly inexplicable behavior patterns.[55] Furthermore, Freud divides the unconscious mind into a threefold system consisting of the "id" (drives and instincts which seek self-satisfaction), the "ego" (interacts with the real world independent of the person), and the "super-ego" (conscience and social norms from childhood).[56]

Third, human drives supply the source of mind energy (hunger, sexual desire, aggression, etc.). Yet, "it is a vulgar misinterpretation of Freud to say that he traced all human behavior to sexual motivations."[57] It is safe to say that for Freud, certain drives acted as mental fuel to fire the behavior of humans.

And fourth, the developmental division represented the influence of childhood experiences on adult life.[58] Freud felt that the full personality was established by the age of five. The depths of the adult life rested in the recesses of the childhood life and experiences.

Freud placed religion on the level of "wish fulfillment." Religion is the attempt to replace the human father with of a divine father. In short, religion prolongs the childish behavior patterns.

> It [religion] too is the product of wish fulfillment. In its monotheistic forms it replaces the fallible father of reality by projecting onto the heavens an omnipotent and infallible father. By this means the status of a child can be retained into adult life. But this is to say that religion perpetuates infantile behavior patterns, notable in relation to guilt and forgiveness. The falsity of religious beliefs is not, of course, entailed by their being the product of wish fulfillment. Freud believed in their falsity on independent grounds. But he thought of religion as a particularly damaging species of illusion, precisely because it militates against the scientific effort to distinguish between what reality in fact is and what we want it to be.[59]

The overall goal of psychoanalysis is self-knowledge. To know the self, one must analyze the general factors that contribute to human nature, be they internal or external. These factors, hidden in the depths of the mind, must be retrieved to correct mental disfunctions.

> This idea that people could suffer from some idea or memory or emotion of which they were not conscious, but from which they could be cured by somehow bringing it into consciousness, is the basis from which Freud's psycho-analysis developed.[60]

Critique of Freud

One of the greatest weaknesses of Freud's system lies in its subjectivity. In other words, Freud's system is safe because any criticism directed toward it could be attributed to some "childhood trauma" of the critic. Stevenson states:

> It [psychoanalysis] certainly has a method of disparagingly analyzing the motivations of its critics (for any questioning of the truth of psycho-analytic theory can be alleged to be based of the unconscious resistance of the critic to its unpleasant implications). So if (as many say) the theory also has a built-in method of explaining away any evidence which appears to falsify it, then it will indeed be a closed system.[61]

Freud's system has a built-in safeguard by which it may dismiss any legitimate criticisms about its own consistency. Bound within its own perceptions of motives and mental causes, the very premises that form psychoanalysis protect it from "negative criticism." Who knows? Perhaps Freud's disrespect for religious truth stems from a childhood memory of falling on the steps of an Austrian cathedral.

Freud's thinking also suffers from a similar fallacy to that of Marx, namely, that society and not man himself is to blame for much of human misery.[62] Again, the "sin nature" of man is attributed to factors outside of man rather than to man himself. Again, in a rationalization for human wickedness, society rather than man is to blame. Freud, like Marx, also relies on a naturalistic world view to sustain his dogmatic attacks upon religious truth. If chemistry and physics are the true test of phenomena, then the question arises: "How many ounces of 'id' and 'ego' fit into a two-gallon test tube?" Such reasoning is merely wishful thinking or, should we say, "wish fulfillment," taken to its logical conclusion.

Jean Paul Sartre: Human Nature with "No Exit"

Jean Paul Sartre (1905-80), the father of modern existentialism, represents one of the best examples of an atheistic growth from the seed of the Enlightenment. For Sartre, God does not exist; thus, man must authenticate himself by taking a volitional "leap of faith" to create his own meaning. Sartre states:

> Atheistic existentialism, which I represent, ... states that if God does not exist, there is at least one being in whom existence precedes essence, a being who exists before he can be defined by any concept, and that this being is man, or as Heidegger says, human reality. What is meant here by saying that existence precedes essence? It means that, first of all, man exists, turns up, appears on the scene, and, only afterwards, defines himself. If man, as the existentialist conceives him, is indefinable, it is because at first, he is nothing. Only afterward will he be something, and he himself will have made what he will be. Thus, there is no human nature, since there is no God to conceive it. Not only is man what he conceives himself to be, but he is also only what he wills himself to be after this thrust toward existence.[63]

From the above, one notes three themes in Sartre's thinking. First, the individual and his being are what is important to Sartre. Theories leave out uniqueness, but ontology encourages it. Second, the meaning or purpose of human life becomes central. The subjective takes on more significance than the objective because there is no objective standard in the universe (i.e., God). And third, freedom represents man's most important and distinctive property. Each person can choose for himself or herself what meaning he or she wishes to give his life. The only basis for values is freedom. All humankind can be sure of is that he or she is there (existence); thus, he or she must choose to give life meaning (essence).

H. STUART ATKINS

Critique of Sartre's Existentialism

The greatest problem of Sartre's thinking rests in the logical ramifications of his view of human freedom. His position, from a logical and functional standpoint, leads to a subjective and relativistic ethic that denies freedom. How is one to determine the degree of freedom allowed for one individual before another individual's freedom is invaded? Freedom for the sake of freedom runs in a relativistic circle. Where is one to draw the line between degrees of freedom if people see such freedom in a relative manner? Jesuit philosopher Dr. Copleston aims at this existentialistic fallacy as he states:

> The validity of the contention that in choosing a value one chooses ideally for all men is perhaps not so clear as Sartre seems to think it is. Is it logically inadmissible for me to commit myself to a course of action without claiming that anyone else in the same situation ought to commit himself in the same way? But his [Sartre's] personally chosen system of ethics could not legitimately be presented as entailed by existentialism, not that is to say, if existentialism illuminates possibilities of choice while leaving the actual choice entirely to the individual.[64]

One wonders what Sartre would think if a team of French university students decided that the ultimate freedom would be the destruction of existentialistic professors. Furthermore, if one claims that freedom is an ethical value, then does not another have the right to claim that the freedom to eliminate freedom is also a value? Yet, if this is done, the very premise of Sartrean thinking becomes a circular logical absurdity.

It seems that existentialistic thinking was perfect for filling the postwar vacuum in the minds of many Europeans. Sartre's thinking may have been more a product of his milieu than a product of truth. With God's existence "assumed" away, the existentialist's only option is to create his own standard: freedom. For the existentialist, a free human rather than a sinful human is the best solution for the problem of evil.

B. F. Skinner and Behavior Modification

During the last quarter of the nineteenth century, psychology adapted the methods of empirical science in the evaluation of human behavior. Men like Wundt of Germany and William James of America studied not the soul or the mind, but instead the "consciousness" of humans. In 1913, J. B. Watson asserted that behavior is the foundation of psychology. From this foundation, Watson asserted that environment, rather than heredity, is the dominant stimulus of behavior. Reflex conditioning is central to behavior. Understandably, Watson denied the reality of unobservable phenomena.

Stemming from Watson's thinking was that of his main disciple, B.F. Skinner (1904-90). Generally, Skinner's thought is bathed in empiricism and naturalistic scientism. For Skinner, only science tells us the truth about human nature.[65] In fact, Skinner goes as far as to assert that science must control the world.[66] He sees religion as a means of manipulating human behavior rather than enhancing it.[67] For Skinner, all human behavior is within the realm of a deterministic framework that shapes human actions and personality. Like the salivation and classical conditioning tests with dogs and birds, man is a servant rather than the master of his environment. Man is thus studied strictly from empirical observation. Man's molder and maker is his environment.

Critique of Skinner's Behaviorism

Certainly, humankind's environment does play a role in shaping his or her behavior, yet the degree to which Skinner stresses this is mistaken. For example, the conclusions reached in experiments with rats and birds cannot be used for specific applications to areas such as government, religion, psychology, economics, and education. Yet Skinner attempts to make such connections.[68] To do so is a classic example of the *post hoc proper hoc* fallacy. Rats and birds may warrant value in basic experimentation, but they are not necessarily the keys to the depths of human behavior. Such reasoning confuses animal instincts with human reasoning and personality.

Skinner, like Marx and Freud, thinks that a change in the environment will result in a changed man.[69] Clearly, the utopian dream through a changed environment is just that: a dream. In many respects, the modern environment has never been better, yet the human condition has never been worse. Who, if scientism is to reign, will choose what is best for all of society—a Pavlovian prince?

Furthermore, to assume that all behavior is determined by causal laws is itself an antiempirical premise. The moment Skinner makes such a statement he transfers his value system into the realm of metaphysics, not science. Thus, he himself falls prey to the "manipulation" of people's thinking through "religious" means. In short, Pavlov's dog implies a logical fog.

Konrad Lorenz and Ethology

In a similar yet quite different vein from that of Skinner, Konrad Zacharias Lorenz (1903-89) leads us to the study of ethology (the comparative study of human and animal behavior). In 1973, Lorenz was awarded a Nobel Prize for physiology and medicine with associates Karl Von Frisch and Nikolaas Tinbergen. Lorenz held the degrees of MD and PhD in zoology from the University of Vienna, Austria.

Lorenz believes that human behavior stems from innate behavior. Through the study of imprinting in very young birds and animals, Lorenz applies his findings to human nature. Evolution, Lorenz believes, supplies the basis of his antibehavioristic position.[70]

Lorenz holds to the three standard premises of evolution: (1) genetics and the traits of parents are passed on to their offspring; (2) mutations bring on the occasional changes in genes, thereby causing variations; (3) "survival of the fittest" explains why certain creatures that survive must possess the strongest traits.

Lorenz thus believes that humankind is an evolved animal. To think of man's origins in any other fashion than evolution would be an illusion for him.[71] Because man is basically an animal, he possesses an innate aggression drive that has been transmitted through the species. Lorenz claims that such a drive is the only explanation for war, which also exhibits the conflict between evolutionary instincts and morality. Furthermore, this aggression trait must be redirected in channels such as art, science, and medicine for it to produce positive rather than negative consequences.[72]

Humor and self-knowledge, according to Lorenz, are the great hopes of the world.

Critique of Lorenz

Lorenz's greatest fallacy rests in the illogical application of animal behavior to that of men. Again, one notes the fallacy of *post hoc proper hoc*. In fact, most of Lorenz's animal experiments are on fish and birds rather than mammals and apes.[74] If applications to human behavior must come from the animal world, certainly "evolutionary cousins" would be the most logical choice. Clearly Lorenz pushes his animal/human analogy to the point of irrationality.

The evolutionary assumptions of Lorenz fail to consider the considerable amount of scientific, logical, and theoretical problems that are inherent in evolution.[75] It seems as if Lorenz attempts to fit human nature into a predetermined evolutionary framework rather than clarifying his superficial and misapplied conclusions. Again, a naturalistic scientism seems to have suppressed the true function of the scientific method.

If man is an animal, there is at least one simple conclusion: he will never be his own God.

Man through the Centuries: What Must We Conclude?

We have briefly traced, from the classical period to the present, a historical survey of how humans evaluate their own nature. In the classical period the motif was *reason*; in the Patristic period it was *revelation*; in the medieval period it was *reason and revelation*; in the Renaissance it was *resurgence and rebirth*; in the Reformation it was *renewal and revelation*; in the Enlightenment it was *naturalism and humanism*; in modern times it is a *renouncement* of human nature and dignity.

Furthermore, in the seven periods of history we have surveyed, certain themes were evident in periods that evidenced inconsistencies concerning human nature, especially as it relates to the problem of evil. First, the denial of a sin nature was evident (classical, parts of the medieval and Renaissance, Enlightenment, and Modern periods). Second, an optimistic and utopian view of human potential was present (classical, Renaissance, Enlightenment, and Modern periods). Third, the attributing of evil to a lack of reason, unbalanced socioeconomic conditions, or wrong choices was prevalent (classical, Enlightenment, and Modern periods). And fourth, a denial of a transcendent and absolute ethical base for man's thoughts and decisions is evident (classical, Enlightenment, and Modern periods).

Plato attempted to solve evil through reason; the Enlightenment through science, humanism, and naturalism; Marx through society; Freud through the mind; Sartre through subjective freedom; Skinner through behavior; and Lorenz through aggression management. Yet, such attempts have still left modern humans with the cold, stark reality of evil.

The preceding "checklist" is not exclusive because certain periods overlap and interrelate in both dates and ideas. But it does serve to drive one to an important conclusion: patristic, medieval, Renaissance, and Reformation thinkers evaluated human nature from a revelational or biblical worldview. Such a worldview aided greatly in the elimination of the five pitfalls from which the five "nonrevelational" periods suffered. Indeed, of these revelational periods, the patristic and the Reformation surface as possessing a most notable anthropology, namely that of biblical theism.

With these thoughts in mind, one final study from our present century will serve as the perfect transition from a historical to a biblical view of human nature.

Dr. Stanton E. Samenow, professor of psychiatry at George Washington University School of Medicine, has written an article in *The Humanist* magazine entitled "The Criminal Personality: New Concepts and New Procedures for Change." In this article, the conclusions of a fifteen-year study on criminal behavior are discussed.

The study, directed by Dr. Samuel Vochelson at Saint Elizabeth's Hospital, Washington, DC, analyzed 255 criminals from all walks of life with hopes of determining reasons for criminal behavior. Dr. Samenow states:

> Our intensive study has a broad base in that its two hundred fifty-five participants come from a variety of backgrounds. Half of the criminals were patients in the forensic psychiatry division at Saint Elizabeth's, and the

rest came to us from the courts and community agencies. Blacks and whites, grade school dropouts and college graduates, criminals from affluent families and those from impoverished families, from the suburbs and from the inner city, from intact homes and from broken homes, were included in the study. In this study of hardcore criminals, almost every category of criminal offense is represented. We have studied the families of many of the criminals at length and have interviewed their friends and employers.[76]

The objective of this study was direct namely, to change criminal behavior. In addition, an attempt was made to understand who the criminal *is*—not just how he acts. Subsequently, it was discovered that changing the *environment* of the criminal was not the answer, but instead a change in the *inner man* is the only hope for changed behavior. Samenow states the central thesis of this study and its findings:

The task of change is much greater than we had ever imagined. *Changing the environment does not change the inner man.* Slums are cleared, job opportunities are offered, schooling is provided, but crime remains. Conventional psychological approaches have failed. After sixteen years of conducting our studies, we do not know what causes crime. What is required is to change the thinking patterns of a lifetime. The criminal must abandon his lifelong patterns of thought and action and learn about a way of life that he has heretofore spurned. He must be habilitated not rehabilitated.[77] [italics my own]

Dr. Samenow goes on to comment on the fallacy of trying to change human nature through environment:

In the 1960's, an era of upheaval and change, it was widely thought that crime was a product of adverse social conditions, whether it was a specific feature of life, such

> as unemployment, or a general condition, such as a "sick
> society." Programs designed to change the environment
> did not alter what a criminal wanted out of life or how
> he functioned in life … what policymakers, lawyers, and
> those who worked with criminals have lacked is a detailed
> knowledge of who the criminal is.[78]

The significance of this study carries vast and powerful implications when one considers that it comes from a modern, humanistic publication. Modern humans, when pushed to the realities of wicked behavior (as seen in the common criminal), are forced to acknowledge that the human problem lies in the inner rather than outer man. Modern secular humans are forced to acknowledge ignorance regarding the origin of crime. In short, this study shows that modern humans, when confronted with their own discoveries concerning human-nature is faced with the anthropology of biblical theism. The real problem with man comes from *within* human nature—not without.

Our task is now to shift from historical anthropology to biblical anthropology. For if God became man through the incarnation, then certainly He is in a most unique position to correctly evaluate human nature.

NOTES

1   Fydor Mikhailovich Dostoevsky, *The Brothers Karamazov*, trans. Andrew H. MacAndrew (Toronto: Bantam Books, 1970), 125.

2   Plato, "Meno," *Classics in Western Philosophy*, ed. Steven M. Cahn (Indianapolis, IN: Hackett, 1977), 19.

3   Frederick Copleston, S. J., *A History of Philosophy*, vol. 1, part 1 (Garden City, NY: Image Books, 1962), 242.

4   Plato, *Republic*, trans. H. D. P. Lee (London: Penguin Books, 1955), 376-412, 521-41.

5   Aristotle, "Nocomachean Ethics," *Classics of Western Philosophy*, ed. Steven M. Cahn (Indianapolis, IN: Hackett, 1977), 175.

6   Copleston, *op. cit.*, vol. 1, part 2, 76.

7   Harold B. Kuhn, "Man, Nature of," *The Zondervan Pictorial Encyclopedia of the Bible*, vol. 4, ed. Merrill C. Tenney (Grand Rapids, MI: Zondervan, 1975), 54.

8   Leslie Stevenson, *Seven Theories of Human Nature* (New York: Oxford University Press, 1974), 33.

9   Kuhn, *op. cit.*, 55.

10   See Philip Schaff, *History of the Christian Church*, vol. 3 (Grand Rapids, MI: Eerdmans, 1910), 802-15; John Ferguson, *Pelagius* (Cambridge: W. Heffer and Sons, 1956).

11   Schaff, *op. cit.*, 816-50.

12   The Stoic view of human nature seems to be a strong element in Pelagianism. This view sees man as inherently good, therefore exempt from the ramifications of the Fall. Furthermore, man can attain self-perfection through self-control. In other words, self-control becomes sin-control. Man, by his own moral efforts, without the aid of any outside source, accomplishes his own "Stoic-salvation." Pelagianism asserts that man himself is capable of a sinless life by a volitional choice. Sinful man becomes superman through his super-will. However, did not the Fall also include the will of man? The Fall of man was not limited to nature but instead encompassed all aspects of the human personality, including the will. Only a sinful man could conclude that he was indeed not sinful. The fact that man claims his sinlessness implies just the opposite. Man's "sinlessness" implies his sinfulness.

13   Schaff, *op. cit.*, 817.

14   *Ibid.*

15   Augustine, *City of God*, trans. Gerald G. Walsh, Demetrius B. Zema, Grace Monahan, and Daniel J. Honan (Garden City, NY: Image Books, 1958), 278-79.

16 "It is commonly said that Augustine Platonized Christianity. This statement must be treated cautiously, for Augustine could not have read many, if any, of Plato's dialogues. In fact, he emphatically rejected many of Plato's most characteristic doctrines, including the doctrines of reincarnation (along with the associated Platonic thesis that the body is the prison of the soul, deserved because of the soul's transgressions in a previous life), recollection (which he replaced with a doctrine of divine illumination), and the denial of moral weakness. Nevertheless, there is a Platonic core to Augustine's thinking. Plato's Forms become for Augustine eternal ideas in God's mind; and, like Plato, Augustine makes a sharp distinction between the things that exist in space or time and that which is outside space and time, the latter being perfect, the former imperfect."[William E. Mann, "Augustine," *Classics of Western Philosophy*, ed. Steven M. Cahn (Indianapolis, IN: Hackett, 1977), 242.]

17 Schaff, *op. cit.*, 841.

18 Kuhn, *op. cit.*, 56.

19 *Ibid*.

20 Schaff, *op. cit.*, vol. 5, 671–72.

21 Copleston, *op. cit.*, vol. 2, part 2, 41.

22 Thomas Aquinas, "The necessity of grace," Q. 109. Art. 2 *Introduction to Saint Thomas Aquinas*, ed. Anton C. Pegis (New York: Random House, 1948), 655.

23 Copleston, *op. cit.*, vol 2, part 2, 20.

24 John Warwick Montgomery, *The Shape of the Past* (Minneapolis, MN: Bethany Fellowship, 1975), 48-49.

25 Desmond Paul Henry, "Medieval Philosophy," *The Encyclopedia of Philosophy*, vol. 5, ed. Paul Edwards (New York: Macmillan, 1967), 253.

26 26. Schaff, *op. cit.*, vol. 6, 559-61.

27 Kuhn, *loc. cit.*

28 *Ibid*.

29 John Warwick Montgomery, *The Shaping of America* (Minneapolis, MN: Bethany House, 1976), 31.

30 Neal W. Gilbert, "Renaissance, "*The Encyclopedia of Philosophy*, vol. 7, ed. Paul Edwards (New York: Macmillan, 1967), 177.

31 Montgomery, *op. cit.*, 118.

32 As quoted in Jerome Blum, Rondo Cameron, and Thomas G. Barnes, *A History; the European World* (Boston: Little, Brown, 1966), 70.

33 *Ibid.*, 65.

34 Schaff, *op. cit.*, vol. 7, vii.

35 *Ibid.*, 3.

36 *Ibid.*, 16.

37 Martin Luther, *Luther's Commentary on Genesis*, vol. 1, trans. J. Theodore Mueller (Grand Rapids, MI: Zondervan, 1958), 73.

38 John Calvin, *Institutes of the Christian Religion*, vol. 1, 3. 14. 1* ed. John T. McNeill (Philadelphia: Westminster Press, 1960), 768-69.

39 Montgomery, *op. cit.*, [in note 24 above], 50-51.

40 Montgomery, *op. cit.*, [in note 29 above], 41-42.

41 Montgomery, *op. cit.*, [in note 24 above], 34.

42 *Ibid.*, 66.

43 Crane Brinton, "Enlightenment," *The Encyclopedia of Philosophy*, vol. 2, ed. Paul Edwards (New York: Macmillan, 1967), 521-22.

44 See Vernon, Venable, *Human Nature: The Marxian View* (New York: Alfred A. Knopf, 1946).

45 Karl Marx, *Karl Marx Selected Writings in Sociology and Social Philosophy*, trans. T. B. Bottomore, ed. T. B. Bottomore and M. Rubel (London: Penguin Books, 1963), 83, cited by Leslie Stevenson, *Seven Theories of Human Nature* (New York: Oxford University Press, 1974), 54.

46 Marx, *Ibid.*, 69, 85.

47 Leslie Stevenson, *Seven Theories of Human Nature* (New York: Oxford University Press, 1974), 48.

48 John Warwick Montgomery, "The Marxist Approach to Human Rights: Analysis and Critique," *Simon Greenleaf Law Review*, 3 (1983-84): 169.

49 Jacques Ellul, *Perspectives on Our Age*, ed., William H. Vanderburg, trans. Joachim Neugroschel (New York: Seabury Press, 1981), 4.

50 See Alexander Solzhenitsyn, "A World Split Apart," *National Review*, JU 78.

51 Harry V. Jaffa, "An Enduring Legacy of Error," *Register*, March 16, 1983, A19.

52 Sigmund Freud, *Two Short Accounts of Psycho-Analysis*, trans. and ed. James Strachey (London: Penguin Books, 1962), 100, cited by Leslie Stevenson, *Seven Theories of Human Nature* (New York: Oxford University Press, 1974), 64.

53 Stevenson, *op. cit.*, 64.

54 Freud, *op. cit.*, 56, 60, 65-66.

55 *Ibid.*, 107, 43, 47.

56 *Ibid.*, 104-5; 137.

57 Stevenson, *op. cit.*, 66.

58 Freud, *op. cit.*, 70, 115.

59 Alasdair Macintyre, "Sigmund Freud," *The Encyclopedia of Philosophy*, vol. 3, ed. Paul Edwards (New York: Macmillan, 1967), 251.

60 Stevenson, *op. cit.*, 62.

61 *Ibid.*, 72.

62 Freud, *op. cit.*, 86-87.

63 Jean Paul Sartre, *Existentialism and Human Emotions* (New York: Philosophical Library, 1957), 15.

64 Copleston, *op. cit.*, vol. 9, part 2, 161-62.

65 B. F. Skinner, *Science and Human Behavior* (New York: Macmillan, 1953), 11, cited in Leslie Stevenson, *Seven Theories of Human Nature* (New York: Oxford University Press, 1974), 94.

66 Skinner, *Ibid.*, 14.

67 *Ibid.*, 350-58.

68 *Ibid.*, 205ff.

69 *Ibid.*, 427-37.

70 Konrad Z. Lorenz, *On Aggression*, trans. Marjorie Latke (London: Methuen University Paperback, 1966), 41, cited by Leslie Stevenson, *Seven Theories of Human Nature* (New York: Oxford University Press, 1974), 110.

71 Lorenz, *Ibid.*, 190-92, 204, 214.

72 *Ibid.*, 243-44.

73 *Ibid.*, 253-57.

74 *Ibid.*, 204.

75 See David N. Livingstone, "Evolution as Metaphor and Myth," *Christian Scholars Review* 12. no. 2, (1983): 111-25.; D. Gareth-Jones, "Man in the Context of Evolutionary Theory," *Horizons of Science*, ed. Carl F. H. Henry, (New York: Harper and Row, 1978), 36-62; Robert E. Kofahl and Kelly L. Segraves, *The Creation Explanation: A Scientific Alternative to Evolution* (Wheaton, IL. : Harold Shaw, 1975); R. L. Wysong, *The Creation-Evolution Controversy (Implications, Methodology and Survey of Evidence) toward a Rational Solution* (Midland, MI: Inquiry Press, 1976.; A. E. Wilder Smith, *Man's Origin, Man's Destiny* (Wheaton, IL: Harold Shaw, 1968).

76 Stanton E. Samenow, "The Criminal Personality: New Concepts and New Procedures for Change," *The Humanist*, September/October 1978, 16.

77 *Ibid.*, 18.

78 *Ibid.*, 18-19.

CHAPTER 2

Anthropology and Evil: A Biblical Survey

Part 2

> In Christianity it is not the eternal man who judges the
> finite man; but the eternal and holy God who judges
> sinful man. Only in a religion of revelation, whose God
> reveals Himself to man from beyond himself and from
> beyond the contrast of vitality and form, can man discover
> the root of sin to be within himself.[1]

In Dr. Samenow's study, "The Criminal Personality: New Concepts and New Procedures for Change," we saw modern man arriving at a similar conclusion to that of biblical Christianity concerning the inner man. Now, a more detailed analysis of biblical anthropology is needed. The proponent of biblical Christianity operates with an essential presupposition always in mind: humankind is sinful. The biblical portrayal of sin is direct, open, and boldly honest concerning human nature. Except for Daniel and Christ, there are no biblical characters who are portrayed as being without sin. The Bible is not afraid to expose even the sinfulness of its central figures (i.e., Adam, Noah, Moses, David, Jonah, and Paul). Biblical theism is realistic, not optimistic, regarding man's nature. Only within the context of redemption does the Christian worldview allow for an optimistic view of human nature.

In place of false optimism, biblical Christianity provides a hope of certainty rather than relativity regarding the problem of evil. Dr. John Laidlaw, in his classic nineteenth century work *The Biblical Doctrine of Man*, asserts:

> The doctrines of the Fall and sin are exclusively biblical ideas; or at least they are only fully conceived and applied in the biblical scheme of religious thought. These doctrines are solvents, not sources of difficulty. Into the problem of evil, Scripture introduces elements of explanation. It accounts for man's present moral and physical condition, for the broad phenomena of life and death, in a way that is thinkable and intelligible. Pascal has said that the Christian faith has mainly two things to establish the corruption of human nature, and its redemption by Jesus Christ. The evil which is in man has been most entirely probed and sounded in connection with that power above man which the gospel brings to his help. We may be asked, why go to a book so simple and practical as the Bible for the solution of the mysterious problems of moral evil, or for any theory of the being of man? We answer that we do so relying upon the surest analogy. It is because revelation has proved such an instrument for man's renovation and recovery to God, because it has achieved the only success in the remedy of man's evil, that we are entitled to expect in it profounder views than anywhere else as to what man and his evils are.[2]

Part 2 now leads us to a brief yet pointed analysis of the Old Testament, New Testament, Christological, and Pauline views of man and his relationship to evil. In addition, one must note that the philosophical basis for the anthropology of biblical theism rests on a most unique foundation: inductive historiography.[3] The assertions of biblical theism are more than just propositions regarding truth, but instead rest on Jesus's claims and support of his deity. The stronghold of Jesus's claim to be God stands on the historical and factual event of the resurrection as recorded in one of the most reliable documents of the ancient world—the New Testament.[4] Because Jesus substantiated his claims to be God through His resurrection, His assertions concerning humans must warrant great attention.[5] Furthermore, to dispense with the truth and authority of biblical theism, one must first attempt a feat never before accomplished by any scholar or individual: a satisfactory refutation of the both the reliability of the New Testament documents and the resurrection of Jesus of Nazareth.[6] If Jesus was indeed God, then the God who became man is in a most unique position to evaluate humanity's greatest needs.

Old Testament Anthropology

One of the most poetic and profound writings regarding the nature of man is found in the books of the Old Testament. In the Pentateuch (the first five books of the Bible), the origin, fall, and beginning history of the nation of Israel and civilization is set forth; in the Wisdom books the poetry of divine wisdom is proclaimed; and in the Prophets the revelation of God is pronounced through chosen men who address the needs of God's people for both the present and the future.

Profundity alone, however, is by no means a valid reason for utilizing the Old Testament as a sound basis for a proper interpretation of human nature. There are valid reasons for concluding that the Old Testament is indeed the inspired Word of God, which addresses its contents with complete accuracy.[7] The late Dr. Gleason Archer, who held the degrees of AB, MA, and PhD from Harvard University, including a BD from Princeton Theological Seminary and an LLB from Suffolk Law School, concludes his chapter on "The Inspiration of the Old Testament," by observing:

> It is foolish and unworthy for one who has been convinced of
> the divine authority of the Bible to question its infallibility
> until each new allegation against it has been cleared up.
> Rather than being a scientific and objective procedure,
> as is sometimes asserted, such a policy involves only an
> illogical shifting from one a priori to another with weak
> minded vacillation. A genuine, outright contradiction in

the Scripture (especially if demonstrable for the original autographs) would be good cause for abandoning faith in the inerrancy of Scripture; but until such has been proved, or until some outright error in history or science has been demonstrated according to the laws of legal evidence, the believer in scripture need never feel embarrassed about holding to the assumption that it is the inerrant Word of God. It is highly significant that no such mistake has ever yet been proved to the satisfaction of a court of law, although various attempts have been made to do so.[8]

Moving from the basis of an inspired Old Testament, four central motifs of Old Testament thought will shape the direction of our analysis. Dr. Alfred Edersheim, the late Grinfield lecturer on the Septuagint at Oxford, summarizes these motifs:

Four great truths, which have their bearing on every part of revelation, come to us from the earliest Scripture narrative, like the four rivers which sprung in the garden of Eden. The first of these truths is the creation of all things by the word of God's power; the second, the descent of all men from our common parents, Adam and Eve; the third, our connection with Adam as the head of the human race, through which all mankind were involved in his sin and fall; and the fourth, that One descended from Adam, yet without his sin, should by suffering free us from the consequences of the Fall, and as the second Adam become the Author of eternal salvation to all who trust in Him.[9]

Creation and the Old Testament

The first of these motifs, God's creative act, places the universe and man in a unique framework. The universe and all it contains is not the equation of chance plus matter but instead was created by a personal God who precisely engineered both matter and man. In fact, the first verse of Genesis begins with the presupposition that God indeed existed before both man and matter. According to Genesis, after creating the natural world, God then created the climax of his works: man. It may even be said that the creation was made for man and not man for the creation. As the prophet Isaiah states in Isaiah 45:18 (NIV).

> For this is what the lord says—he who created the heavens, he is God; he who fashioned and made the earth, he founded it; he did not create it to be empty, but formed it to be inhabited—he says: "I am the LORD, and there is no other."

Man's beginning is thus not based on a random, chance accident of the cosmos. Instead, man is the highest creation of the personal God of the universe, who, with design, intent, and purpose, formed man's body out of the base elements of the earth and molded man's soul after His own image. Man is not the product of chance—man is the creation of the God of the Bible. God thus creates man in "His image" and places him in the Garden of Eden. The perfect environment, alongside the perfect inner man is now set to usher in society. Edersheim states:

> Of all His works God only, Gen. 1:27, KJV, "created man in His own image in the image of God created He him." This expression refers not merely to the intelligence with which God endowed, and the immortality with which He gifted man, but also to the perfect moral and spiritual nature which man at the first possessed. And all his surroundings were in accordance with his happy state. In Gen. 2:15, KJV, God "put him into the garden of Eden to dress it and to keep it," and gave him a congenial companion in Eve, whom Adam recognized as bone of his bones, and flesh of his flesh.[10]

Adam, Eve, and the Old Testament

From the creation of the cosmos and man, the relation of Adam and Eve to the human race is also relevant. That all of humanity can trace their "roots" to Adam and Eve is an essential fact of the Old Testament. Indeed, "the OT sees the human race as having sprung from a common origin, and as being the progeny of a single primal pair."[11] Furthermore, from the descendants of the post-fall Adam and Eve, one notes the rapid spread of the Fall's consequences.[12] Murder was quick to spread, and the human race was merely an infant when the deadly results of sin were present. For, "Adam had, so to speak, broken the first great commandment, Cain the first and second; Adam had committed sin, Cain both sin and crime."[13] Mankind was now on a collision course with the results of its own personal and corporate rebellion.

The Fall: Biblical and Extrabiblical Evidence

In addition to Adam and Eve as the parental basis of mankind, their fall provides the sinful origin of human nature. To deny the Fall is essentially to deny the core of man's nature: sin. For, the reality of such a fall is not an isolated and internal account of the Old Testament. Significant, external evidence exists from other cultures and oral traditions that parallel the Old Testament fall account. For example, British anthropologist the late E. K. Victor Pearce, who held degrees in anthropology from Oxford and the University of London, in his classic work *Who Was Adam?*, states at length:

> There is another source which has been drawn upon as evidence for the Fall. This is the myths of primitive peoples handed down orally from generation to generation, long before contact with Western civilization. Many social anthropologists think this evidence is significant.
>
> Dr. Zwemer says: "The evidence of anthropology therefore seems to be that of an almost universal tradition of a creation of the world by a High-God in which man occupies a special place as its culmination. Moreover, we find together with this account of man's place in the universe and parallel to it a widely-spread tradition of man's displacement of a tragedy of disobedience and the loss of his former state of happiness. Who can resist the conclusion that these many and multiform creation-myths, these constant memories

of a lost 'age of innocence' point to a common human tradition and corroborate the scriptural data?"

These myths are called the "world views" of primitive peoples. F. M. Savina reports the world view of original inhabitants of China called the Miao: "The Miao hold an essentially monotheistic faith, they have never had a written language, they live in tribes and are an ancient people, having inhabited China before the present Chinese, and been pushed by them towards the mountains in the south. They believe in a Supreme Being, Creator of the world and of men. Death came as a consequence of man's sin: the woman had eaten white strawberries forbidden by the lord of Heaven. They know of a deluge, followed by a dispersal of peoples."

J. A. MacCulloch reports on the Andamanese who are a preliterate and technologically simple people: "The Andamanese, whose remarkable theology, according to the best authorities, is independent of Christian influence, believe that Puluga, the creator, gave the first man, Tomo, various injunctions, especially concerning certain trees which grew only at one place (Paradise) in the jungle, and which he was not to touch at certain seasons—during the rains, when Puluga himself visits them and partakes, later, some of Tomo's descendants disobeyed and were severely punished. Others, disregarding Puluga's commands about murder, adultery, theft, etc., and becoming more and more wicked, were drowned in a deluge. Two men and two women survived, and in revenge wished to kill Puluga, who, telling them their friends had been justly punished, disappeared from the earth."[14]

The significance of the above evidence is astounding when one notes that, independent of any "Judeo-Christian" influence, cultures exist with oral traditions that match the biblical account of the creation and fall of man.[15] How, one must ask, could cultures that are separated by geography, language, and time span possess matching accounts of a very descriptive, historical account? In fact, the chances of two independent cultures expounding such events are minimal, especially when minute themes and details exist in the same story. Moreover, the existence of oral tradition in nonliterate cultures does not guarantee the precise transmission of oral themes and details. From generation to generation, details may be added and deleted. But with the Old Testament, one can establish the fact and tradition of the origin and fall of man on grounds that can be verified historically, textually, traditionally, and with additional support as recorded by Christ and the apostles in the New Testament. On top of such a basis, we have noted cultures that are separate of Judeo-Christian influence, yet possess identical accounts to those which are recorded in Genesis. Does this not suggest that at one time humankind existed in a common culture (from which the consistency of these stories derive their source), which at some point in ancient history was dispersed? Perhaps akin to the tower of Babel? Furthermore, does not consistent and parallel accounts of an event from separate cultures serve to verify such an event? Even modern anthropology, as noted by E. K. Pearce, attests to the importance of this evidence. The reality of the Fall does indeed rest on both biblical and extrabiblical records. For one to believe otherwise, both the findings of modern anthropology and a historically reliable Old Testament would have to be ignored.

Genesis and the Fall Account

In light of the varied cultural and biblical consensus on the Fall of man, one must now shift to the most specific record of the Fall: the Genesis account of Adam and Eve's rebellion.

As a result of their eating of the forbidden fruit, the strongest summation of the Old Testament view of human nature arises in Genesis 6:5 (NIV) and 8:21 (NIV). There it states:

> The Lord saw how great man's wickedness on the earth had become, and that every inclination of the thoughts of his heart was only evil all the time. Never again will I curse the ground because of man, even though every inclination of his heart is evil from childhood.

Some observations must now be made. First, these passages assert that the heart of humanity is not in a mild state of hedonism. Humans' sinful nature places them in an *extreme* state of evil, wickedness, and depravity. The consequences of the Fall warrant strong and continuous adjectives for describing humans' post-Fall status. No middle ground is available. Sin is sin. To say otherwise is to ignore or rationalize the reality of biblical and human experience. Or, as the late Dr. Franz Delitzsch writes concerning Genesis 6:5: "The Character of the picture is as dark as possible."[16] Second, an assertion is made that sin starts its process not as a series of "mistakes" that one makes in response to his or her environment, but instead finds its fetal origins as a result of the passage of sin from generation to generation. This is not to say that sin is therefore Adam's fault rather than his ancestors. The issue is that man, through his past and present choice, is both related to and responsible for the sin of Adam himself. The late Dr. Robert Gordis, professor of Bible and Rapaport Professor of the Philosophies of Religion at Jewish Theological Seminary of America, writes:

> It would be impossible for a Hebrew thinker to conceive of the idea that God is responsible for man's sinfulness or even his proclivity to sin. That man is free to choose the right is the bedrock of biblical ethics. The lawgiver in Deuteronomy enjoins: "Behold I have placed before you today life and the good, and death and the evil. Life and death have I placed before you, the blessing and the curse. You shall choose life, so that you may live, you and your children" (Deut. 30:16-19, KJV; cf. 11:26ff, KJV.). This thrice-repeated injunction is echoed throughout the Hebrew Bible by prophet and sage alike.[17]

Who is there among mankind that could cast the first stone against Adam?

The late Dr. Kyle M. Yates, professor of Old Testament at Baylor University, maintains concerning Genesis 6:5:

> Wickedness (*ra'at*)repented (*naham*) grieved (*'asab*). The depravity was widespread. And it was inward, continual,

and habitual. Man was utterly corrupt, bad in heart and in conduct. There was no good in him. The whole bent of his thoughts and imaginations was completely out of line with the will of Jehovah. Flesh was on the throne. God was forgotten or openly defied. Naham in the niphal form describes the love of God that has suffered heartrending disappointment. Literally, it speaks of taking a deep breath in extreme pain. God's purposes and plans had failed to produce the precious fruit that he had anticipated, because sinful man had prevented their full fruition. 'Asab in the hithpail form means to pierce oneself or to experience piercing. The statement says, then, that God experienced heart-piercing sorrow as he looked upon the tragic devastation sin had produced. His handiwork had been marred and ruined. Through it all, God's love shone clearly, even when the rumblings of divine judgement began to threaten the people of the earth.[18]

The Old Testament thus sees evil not as a superficial and dualistic opposite of good but instead as the consequence of human rebellion through the abuse of free will. The Dr. Jekyll of the garden has shifted to the Mr. Hyde of sinful rebellion. No longer is the *imago deo* the predominant characteristic of humans. Instead, human sin nature attempts to overcome the "God nature."

Edersheim summarizes the despair and hope of the Fall:

After the fall the position of man towards God was entirely changed. In the garden of Eden man's hope of being confirmed in his estate and of advancing upwards depended on his perfect obedience. But man disobeyed and fell.[19]

It is to the role of a Deliverer that we now must turn.

The Old Testament Promise of Redemption

The highlight of Old Testament anthropology lies not in the reality of man's sin, but more so in the promise of the one who will eliminate such sin. Although the Old Testament view of man is bleak, it does point to an anthropological restoration through the promised messiah—Jesus of Nazareth.[20] Regarding this redemptive hope, Edersheim states:

> When our first parents left the garden of Eden, it was not without hope, nor into outer darkness. They carried with them the promise of a Redeemer, the assurance of the final defeat of the great enemy, as well as the Divine institution of a Sabbath on which to worship, and of the marriage-bond by which to be joined together into families. Thus the foundations of the Christian life in all its bearings were laid in Paradise.[21]

Coupled with man's curse was also man's cure in Christ. Jesus of Nazareth, who was both God and man, is in the perfect position to redeem and thus recover humans. The Old Testament did not leave humans hopeless concerning their sin but instead pointed consistently to one who will bring hope concerning sin. In fact, modern man has much to learn from the redemptive focus of the Old Testament message. As the late Reinhold Niebuhr has so insightfully written in his work *The Nature and Destiny of Man*:

> The very fact that the strategies of redemption are in such complete contradiction to each other proves how far modern man is from solving the problem of evil in his life.[22]

Fortunately, the biblical strategy of redemption offers us hope rather than modern hopelessness. We must now turn to the "Blessed Hope" of New Testament anthropology.

H. STUART ATKINS

New Testament Anthropology

The New Testament view of man, based on the Old Testament record of man's Fall, centers around two motifs: man's sinfulness and Christ's redemption. In addition, the overall anthropology of the Gospels is not in the form of a detailed analysis of human nature but instead takes its shape primarily in the parables and interaction of Christ with individuals and twenty-five groups.[23]

Jesus, in his statements about human nature, proclaims the exact view of man as found in the Old Testament—namely that man is sinful and in vast need of redemption. In fact, Jesus even addresses his own disciples as sinful.[24] Furthermore, Christ also proclaimed that man's warped nature stems from the inner man. The deepest recesses of man are affected by sin.[25] Jesus asserted his epistemological certainty regarding man's inner nature.[26] Jesus spoke of sin in specific rather than abstract terms.[27] As a summation of the Gospel's account of man, Dr. Kuhn states:

> The four gospels thus portray man—seen through the eyes of Jesus Christ—as having suffered an original catastrophe which cast its long and melancholy shadow across human experience and human history. The nature of man thus bore the disastrous effects of the fall; but as a foil to this, it was made clear that mankind possessed a residual capacity for sonship with God through grace.[28]

In contrast to the Gospels, the book of Acts portrays the new nature which a believer possesses from the point of salvation.[29] Although the book of Acts did not ignore the wickedness of man,[30] it did show the anthropological ramifications of a redemptive transformation through salvation in Christ.

The Pauline View of Man

The most specific and pointed view of man in the New Testament is represented by Paul's anthropology in the book of Romans. In Romans 5:12-31, Paul sets forth his classic exposition on the sinful nature of man as related to Adam. Because of the vast importance of this passage, a brief exegesis is needed to best understand the Pauline view of man.

The first exegetical approach in analyzing this passage focuses on the context which precedes Romans. In Romans 1:1-17, Paul writes of God's salvation for sinners. He then, in Romans 1:18-3:20, speaks of God's holiness in condemning sin, and in chapters 3:21-5:21, develops the theme of God's grace in justifying sinners.[31] Consequently, the specific context also possesses the theme of sin and its relation to man's condition. In fact, Romans 5:12 is sandwiched between fifteen verses that stress the correlation of Adamic sin with man's sin. Hence, within both the general and specific context of Romans 5, the central thrust deals with one issue: man and his sinfulness.

Second, the logical flow of thought in Romans 5 establishes a direct connection between the sin of Adam and the sin of humankind. Here Paul utilizes a technique that progresses from specific to general. For example, "the one the many," and its general concept, is used in at least 50 percent of the verses from 5:12 to 5:21 (NASB). In verses 12, 15, 16, and 18, Paul consistently drives home the correlation between Adam's sin and its direct effect on humankind. The one equals Adam; the many equals post-Adamic man. Hence, mankind is engulfed in a sinful solidarity of depravity that stems from Adam to all of humanity. Dr. John Murray, educated in Glasgow, Edinburgh, and Princeton, and formerly professor of systematic theology at Westminster Theological Seminary, writes:

> The most conclusive refutation of the view in question is the explicit and repeated affirmations of the context to the effect that condemnation and death reign over all because of the *one sin* of the *one man* Adam. On at least five occasions in verses 15-19 this is asserted. This reiteration establishes beyond doubt that the apostle regarded condemnation and death as having passed on to all men by the one trespass of the one man Adam. This sustained appeal to the one sin of the one man rules out the possibility of construing it as equivalent to the actual personal transgressions of countless individuals.[32]

Indeed, the sin of Adam was also the sin of "the many."

Third, a grammatical analysis of a specific Greek clause is of vital importance in arriving at the central meaning of this passage. The clause in question is the last phrase in Romans 5:12 (NASB) which states: "because all sinned." At first glance, this clause seems insignificant, but the general interpretation of this passage hinges on this one clause. For example, the Pelagian interpretation of verse 12 would assert that it is an unfinished comparison (containing the protasis without the apodosis), yet such an interpretation fails to notice the completion of this comparison in verses 13 and following.[33] Moreover, this clause should not be translated as a coordinating conjunction ("in whom"), but instead as a causative conjunction. Bauer, Arndt, and Gingrich specifically list this clause (*eph'ho*), under the following definition: "of that upon which a state of being, an action, or a result is based."[34] Therefore, this clause is best translated: "for this reason that all sinned," thus establishing a causative relationship between the sin of Adam, referred to in the first part of this verse, and the sin of mankind, referred to in this clause and the following verses. This in turn forms a direct correlation in support of man's sinfulness. Dr. Murray writes:

> There can be no question but the fact that 'all sinned' is stated in the most explicit fashion to be the ground upon which death penetrated to all man, just as the sin of Adam is the reason why death entered the world.[35]

Fourth, additional passages of scripture also seem to support man's inherent sinfulness. Note the following passages:

> What is man, that he should be pure, or he who is born of a woman, that he should be righteous. (Job 15:14 NASB)

> Behold, I was brought forth in iniquity, and in sin my mother conceived me. (Psalm 51:5 NASB)

> The wicked are estranged from the womb; These who speak lies go astray from birth. (Psalm 58:5 NASB)

Among them we too all formerly lived in the lusts of our
flesh, indulging the desires of the flesh and of the mind,
and were by nature children of wrath, even as the rest.
(Ephesians 2:3 NASB)

From the above passages, one notes that three of these four connect sin
with human birth or the womb. The fourth verse refers to human nature,
which implies an inherent, not an actual, condition. To assert therefore
that humankind is not sinful at birth in essence is to ignore four clear
passages of scripture that teach that he is. If sin is merely actual, what must
be done with the preceding verses?

The apostle Paul was no stranger to the reality of human sin. In fact,
in Romans 7:20 (NASB) Paul correlates volition with sin as he proclaims:
"But if I am doing the very thing I do not wish, I am no longer the one
doing it, but sin which dwells in me." Sin, thus, in Pauline theology is
central, but the cross and its effect on sin is essential. The late Dr. William
Hamilton, William Newton Clarke Professor of Christian Theology and
Ethics at Colgate Rochester Divinity School, writes:

A good bit of Paul's time in Romans is given over to his
analysis of the reality of sin. All men are involved, both
Gentile and Jew (1:18-2:24); sin is universal. Sometimes
he treats this as an empirical fact, sometimes he tries to
explain it (as in 5:12-19, where he traces it to Adam). Even
the man in Christ knows the struggle against sin (Rom.
7:7-25). But as we look at the transition between Chapters
7 and 8 in Romans one thing is clear. If sin has been a
leading character in the story of salvation up to the cross,
after this event it no longer plays a major role. With the
coming of Christ, it is there, but in the shadows. It is
present, but it no longer has the power to determine the
outcome of the story.[36]

Conclusion

Unlike the study of criminal behavior in our closing remarks concerning a historical survey of man, biblical theism asserts the cause of crime. Man's major problem does come from the inner man (sin), yet the solution arises from a divine transformation of the inner man through Christ Himself. The apostle Paul in 2 Corinthians 5:17 (NASB) states: "Therefore, if any man is in Christ, he is a new creature; the old things passed away; behold, new things have come."

Much of the problem of evil is a result of human nature rather than a "contradiction" in God's nature. Biblical theism does not just pontificate answers to evil and suffering; rather it provides a solution that changes man from the inside out. Yet this change is hardly an argument from "religious experience." The central cure for human evil—the life, death, and resurrection of Christ—shouts forth as an authentic historical fact that separates biblical theism from all the world's religions. If sin is the major cause of the problem of evil, and Christ died on the cross to render sin powerless, then did not Christ solve the problem of evil? Granted, this still leaves room for further clarification and discussion, but at least biblical theism supplies both an origin and a solution to evil and suffering.

Biblical theism also supplies man with some distinctives, which renders it unique among solutions to the problem of evil. First, there is the infinite, personal Creator who fashioned man in His image. Second, there exists a balance between man and his dignity and man and his fallen nature. Third, God did not wait passively by as evil progressed amid humankind, but instead God became man through His Son, Jesus Christ (incarnation). Fourth, God Himself suffered on the cross so that humans might have complete freedom from sin and evil (redemption). And fifth, an eschatological hope remains as Christ will one day return to create a new heaven and a new earth.

The late Dr. Francis A. Schaeffer, a philosopher, theologian, and author, and C. Everett Koop, the former surgeon general of the United States, will serve as a final reminder of biblical theism's position on human nature and its relationship to evil and suffering:

> The Bible tells us also, however, that man is flawed. We
> see this to be the case both within ourselves and in our

societies throughout the world. People are noble and people are cruel; people have heights of moral achievement and depths of moral depravity.

But this is not simply an enigma, nor is it explained in terms of "the animal in man." The Bible explains how man is flawed, without destroying the uniqueness and dignity of man. Man is evil and experiences the results of evil, not because man is non-man but because man is fallen and thus is abnormal.

The Fall brought not only moral evil but also the abnormality of (1) each person divided from himself or herself; (2) people divided from other people; (3) mankind divided from nature; and (4) nature divided from nature. This was the consequence of the choice made by Adam and Eve sometime after the Creation. It was not any original deformity that made them choose in this way. God had not made them robots, and so they had real choice. It is man, therefore, and not God, who is responsible for evil.

Christians do not see things as if they always have been this way. This is of immense importance in understanding evil in the world. It is possible for Christians to speak of things as absolutely wrong, for they are not original in human society. They are derived from the fall; they are in that sense "abnormal." It also means we can stand against what is wrong and cruel without standing against God, for He did not make the world as it now is.[37]

With our discussion of ontology and anthropology behind us, we must now move to one of the most profound works the world has ever known regarding evil and suffering: the book of Job. Personified in Job is a specific example of how one must react to evil when *all* the answers to theodicy are not apparent and immediate.

NOTES

1   Reinhold Niebuhr, *The Nature and Destiny of Man; A Christian Interpretation*, vol. 1, *Human Nature* (London: Nisbet, 1941), 17-18.

2   John Laidlaw, *The Biblical Doctrine of Man* (Edinburgh: T.&T. Clark, 1895), 200-201.

3   For an excellent argument concerning the verification and significance of the historical basis to biblical theism, see John Warwick Montgomery, "The Quest for absolutes: An Historical Argument," *Jurisprudence: A Book of Readings*, ed. John Warwick Montgomery (Strasbourg, France: International Scholarly Publishers, 1974), 527-29.

4   Sir Frederic Kenyon, who was the director and principal librarian of the British Museum, and considered one of greatest authorities on classical manuscripts, writes the following concerning the New Testament manuscripts: "The interval then between the dates of original composition and the earliest extant evidence becomes so small as to be in fact negligible, and the last foundation for any doubt that the Scriptures have come down to us substantially as they were written has now been removed. Both the *authenticity* and the general *integrity* of the books of the New Testament may be regarded as finally established." [Frederic G. Kenyon, *The Bible and Archaeology* (New York and London: Harper & Row, 1940], 288-89? Kenyon's underline, cited in John Warwick Montgomery, *Where Is History Going* (Minneapolis, MN: Bethany House, 1969), 45.]

5   Dr. Norman Geisler, professor of philosophy of religion at Dallas Theological Seminary, says of the resurrection: "Now in view of the prediction of the resurrection, the event is given special confirming significance." Karl Popper argued that whenever a "risky prediction" is fulfilled, it counts as confirmation of the hypothesis which comes with it. If so, what could be a riskier prediction than a resurrection? and hence, what could have greater confirmational force than the resurrection of Christ? If a man would not accept a predicted resurrection as evidence of a truth claim, then he has an unfalsifiable bias against the truth (cf. Luke 16:31)."[Norman Geisler, *Christian Apologetics* (Grand Rapids, MI: Baker Book, 1976), 347.]

6   For examples of agnostics and atheists that reversed their thinking because of the evidence for Christ's resurrection and deity, see Josh McDowell, *Evidence That Demands a Verdict; Historical Evidences for the Christian Faith* (San Bernardino, CA: Here's Life Publishers, 1972), 355-57.

7   For a defense of the inspiration of the Old Testament, see the following works: R. K. Harrison, *Introduction to the Old Testament* (Grand Rapids,

MI: Eerdmans, 1969), 462-75; Gleason L. Archer, "The Inspiration of the Old Testament," *A Survey of Old Testament Introduction* (Chicago: Moody, 1964), 19-34; J. W. Montgomery, *Crisis in Lutheran Theology* (Grand Rapids, MI: Eerdmans, 1967), 15-44; M. H. Woudstra, "The Inspiration of the Old Testament," *The Bible: The Living Word of God*, ed. Merrill C. Tenney (Grand Rapids, MI: Zondervan, 1968), 123-42.

8   Gleason L. Archer, "The Inspiration of the Old Testament," *A Survey of Old Testament Introduction* (Chicago: Moody, 1964), 33-34.

9   Alfred Edersheim, *Old Testament Bible History*, vol. 1 (Grand Rapids, MI: Eerdmans, 1979), 17.

10   Edersheim, *Ibid.*, 20.

11   Harold B. Kuhn, "Man, Nature Of," *The Zondervan Pictorial Encyclopedia of the Bible*, vol. 4, ed. Merrill C. Tenney (Grand Rapids, MI: Zondervan, 1975), 50.

12   For a detailed study of Rabbinic Judaism and its treatment of the problem of evil, see A. P. Hayman, "Rabbinic Judaism and the Problem of Evil," *Scottish Journal of Theology* 29, no. 5 (1976): 461-76.

13   Edersheim, *op. cit.*, 25.

14   E. K. Victor Pearce, *Who Was Adam?* (Great Britain: Paternoster, 1969), 71-72.

15   The following cultures have a full concept of the biblical idea of man's transgression: Assyrio-Babylonia 1, Syria, Egypt, Italy, Lithuania, India, Lenni Lenape (US), Takoe (US), Leeward Islands, Fiji Islands 2, Andaman Island, and Hawaii. The following two cultures and traditions have a partial concept of man's transgression or sinfulness: Persia 2 and Thlinkut (Canada) 1. [Cited from John Warwick Montgomery, *The Quest for Noah's Ark*, 2nd rev. ed. (Minneapolis, MN: Bethany House, 1974), 33.]

16   Franz Julius Delitzsch, *A New Commentary on Genesis* vol. 1 trans. Sophia Taylor (London: T.&T. Clark, 1888), 233.

17   Robert Gordis, *The Book of God and Man: A Study of Job* (Chicago: University of Chicago Press, 1965), 62.

18   Kyle M. Yates, "Genesis," *The Wycliffe Bible Commentary*, eds. Charles F. Pfeiffer and Everett F. Harrison (Chicago: Moody, 1962), 12.

19   Edersheim, *op. cit.*, 27.

20   See Josh McDowell, *Evidence That Demands A Verdict* (San Bernardino, CA: Here's Life, 1972), 141-77.

21   Edersheim, *op. cit.*, 22.

22   Niebuhr, *op. cit.*, 25.

23   Kuhn, *op. cit.*, 51.

24   Luke 11:13 (NASB).

25   Matt. 15:11, 19-20 (NASB); Mark 7:21-23 (NASB).

26   John 2:25 (NASB).

27   Millar Burrows, *An Outline of Biblical Theology* (Philadelphia: Westminster, 1946), 167.

28   Kuhn, *op. cit.*, 52.

29   Acts 4:32; 9:1, 2; 9:27-29; 22:3-6 (NASB).

30   Acts 24:25-27.

31   Irving L. Jensen's outline of Romans, quoted from syllabus, BIB. 203, Columbia Bible College, 1980.

32   John Murray, *The Epistle to the Romans*, ed. F. F. Bruce, *The New International Commentary on the New Testament* (Wm. B. Eerdmans, Grand Rapids, MI, reprint edition, 1980), 183-84.

33   *Ibid.*, 182.

34   William F. Arndt and F. Wilbur Gingrich, trans. *A Greek-English Lexicon of the New Testament and Other Early Christian Literature*, (Chicago: University of Chicago Press, 1979.) 287.

35   Murry, *op. cit.*, 182.

36   William Hamilton, "A Theology for Modern Man," *The Nature of Man in Theological and Psychological Perspective*, ed. Simon Doniger (New York: Harper & Brothers, 1962), 232.

37   C. Everett Koop and Francis A. Schaeffer, *Whatever Happened to the Human Race?* (Westchester, IL: Crossway Books, 1979), 109-10.

CHAPTER 3

The Book of Job: Innocent Suffering and the Justice of God

> The Book of Job is not an abstract argument, a cold debate, a sentimental play, a Virgil's Aeneid, a Homer's Iliad, a Goethe's Faust, a Shakespeare's Macbeth. Its greatest mission is not to display poetic beauty, or to create sublime literature, or to potentate human genius. Its chief design is not to offset foreign philosophy, or to correct current views. Some of these things are evidently implied. Its chief purpose is more noble, more lofty. It is full of war, full of struggle, full of ethics, full of life. Divinity and humanity are its counterparts; holiness and sinfulness, its struggling phases; God and man, its chief subjects; a world governed and a world suffering, its profound questions.[1]

Standing as one of four great literary works of the world, the book of Job towers with truth and strength as it addresses the problem of evil. Men such as Carlyle, Tennyson, and Immanuel Kant were just a few of the thinkers who seriously absorbed and respected the profundity of Job. Faced with the justice of God on the one hand and the reality of his innocent suffering on the other, Job features a story bathed with both the limitations of man and the mysteries of God.

Thus far in chapters 1 and 2, we have discussed the results of sin as it applies to the problem of evil, yet Job takes us to the next logical question:

Why must the innocent suffer? In an age so flooded with the despair and results of evil, Job supplies an ancient light that shines amid the gloom of contemporary man's problems. Dr. Robert Gordis states:

> The evils confronting our age are not exhausted by this complex of potential disasters on the world arena. Virtually every country in the East or in the West, newly developing or highly industrialized, exhibits a widespread breakdown of moral standards in personal life, in commerce and industry, in education and government. The large-scale practice of violence, the acceptance of lying as an indispensable technique for success, and the callous suppression of the rights of the weak and the poor go hand in hand with the far-flung hypocrisy through which men express their loyalty to ideals that they trample under foot in practice.

> The ubiquity of evil and its apparent triumph everywhere give particular urgency to the most agonizing riddle of human existence, the problem of evil, which is the crucial issue in biblical faith. But the tempo of change today is far too hectic and modern man is all too little disposed to take spiritual inventory of his situation. Our activistic, frantic age is not an era of meditation.

> Nevertheless, more and more sensitive men and women, whether rooted in some religious tradition or in none, have wrestled in the night with the demon of doubt and despair; for many the dawning of a new faith in life and its Giver has not yet come. In this far-flung quest, which takes on untold forms, many men, women, and young people have turned to the book of Job as a precious resource for grappling with the problem of evil. Never has this book, the most profound and—if such an epithet may be allowed—the most beautiful discussion of the theme, been more relevant than in our age, when man's suffering

has exceeded his wildest nightmares, in this, the most brutal of centuries.[2]

The central focus of the book of Job is as follows: man, in his finite and limited knowledge, must humbly bow before the infinite, personal, sovereign, just, and omnipotent God, regardless of the perplexing "contradictions" of an evil world. Mankind must thus learn to respond to suffering in a manner identical to Job's obedience and example.

In our study of Job, we shall briefly cover the background, outline, concept of justice, and some lessons of Job. This study will adhere to a survey of the central themes of Job rather than a critical exposition and commentary of Job.

General Background of Job

Concerning the name Job ('*Iyyob*, in Hebrew), there are three possible sources pertaining to the etymology of the name. First, from the Hebrew, it most likely comes from a root that means to come back or repent. Second, another possible meaning for the word *Job* would be the assailed one ('*ayeb*, in Hebrew), which also means to hate or be at enmity. And third, Arabic spells the name '*Awwabun*, which is found in Akkadian works. Regarding this Arabic etymology, one must note that because Job was a native of North Arabia, in addition to the Arabic flavor of the book of Job, such an Arabic connection may be important.[3]

The first chapter of Job mentions that Job was from the geographic location called the land of Uz. The exact location of this region is not known, yet an educated guess is within reach. According to the late Dr. Elmer B. Smick, professor of Old Testament languages and literature at Gordon-Conwell Theological Seminary, "Uz might have been the name of a wide region encompassing many tribes East of Palestine from Edom to Aram."[4]

From the geography of Job, one must then shift to the most significant background information of Job: the date of composition. Although there are vast opinions regarding the date of composition for Job, a distinction should be made between the event itself and the record of such an event. Often, an event happens, then it is later recorded with no specific indication as to when the actual event occurred. With the book of Job, there is evidence for both an ancient event and composition.

Summoning evidence for an early second millennium dating of Job, Dr. Archer summarizes the findings of William E. Albright, one of the world's foremost Old Testament archaeologists:

> W. P. Albright in his chapter on the "Old Testament and Archaeology" in the Alleman and Flack Commentary indicates that the historical Job may well have been contemporary with the patriarchs. His basis for this conclusion rests partly upon the dubious ground that Ezekiel 14:14 couples the names of Job and Daniel. Albright understands this Daniel to be the ancient Canaanite here Daniel, who appears as a prominent figure in one of the Ugaritic epics, that is, as the idol-worshiping father of Ahata. Thus he rejects the possibility that Ezekiel could be referring to this own contemporary, Daniel, in Babylon. He also points out the fact that the other names in the narrative are authentic for the second millennium B.C. Thus, Bildad was probably shortened from Yabildadum, a name found in cuneiform sources dating from that period. He also traces a noteworthy resemblance to the account of the "Babylonian Job," a cuneiform composition translated in Barton's AB. This is the story of a righteous man who underwent the bitterest agony of body and spirit, even though he was conscious of having lived an upright life, and nevertheless remained steadfast in the midst of his affliction. Ultimately, he was granted a happier life than ever, to the glory of Marduk, the god of Babylon. This Babylonian account may go back to 1200 BC and may rest upon materials even earlier.[5]

Evidence for an ancient composition of Job is also substantial. Overall, five options in dating result: (1) age of the patriarchs, (2) Solomon's reign, (3) Manasseh's reign, (4) Jeremiah's generation, (5) exilic or postexilic period.[6]

In consideration of the above five options, the first two carry the strongest support. Concerning the first dating, both the Talmud and the general consensus of the Christian scholars until modern times supports a pre-Mosaic dating.[7] As for the second dating, evidence in support for this period is significant, yet it could also apply to an earlier date, especially if Job was written by a non-Israelite author in a non-Israelite location.[8]

To date the book of Job during later periods (sixth to second centuries BC), ignores an essential fact of Job's text: there are no references to Moses, the twelve tribes, or the patriarchal system.[9] Archer writes:

> Only in Job is there a complete absence of such references. [To the Israelite monarchy] This striking factor by itself renders all of the late-date theories of the composition of Job completely at variance with the internal evidence of the text itself. This total ignorance of Israel on the part of a culture so close to the borders of Israel subsequent to Joshua's conquest, points unmistakably to the period of the Egyptian sojourn (1876-1445 B.C.) as the most likely period for the origin of Job.[10]

Hence, Job could well be the oldest book in the Bible. God thus saw the importance of dealing with the "chief stumbling block to all men's faith in the goodness and power of God as the ruler and judge over all the world."[11] It seems that God, through the book of Job, supplied a preface on suffering for the rest of history. In his omniscience and sovereignty, God was fully aware of the perplexity man would face as he witnessed and experienced suffering; thus, by divine inspiration through a human author, God used the book of Job as a precedent for dealing with evil and suffering. In other words, God gave biblical answers before man even asked the questions.

Integrity of the Text of Job

If one adheres to the conclusions of modern documentary criticism, the text of Job is said to be "probably more corrupt than that of any other biblical book."[12] However, such a conclusion is more the result of presupposition than fact. The evidence for the textual integrity of Job is far from "corrupt" when the textual evidence (rather than presuppositions) is allowed to speak for itself. Furthermore, a textual problem does not necessitate a textual "mistake," especially when all the evidence is not yet available. The late Dr. Francis I. Anderson, MA, BD, MSC, PhD, and DD, who was a research fellow with the Australian Institute of Archaeology, asserts the following concerning the text of Job:

> The incomplete state of our research should not be permitted to diminish our respect for the integrity of the Hebrew text. On the contrary, the difficulties we encounter are themselves a tribute to the fidelity of the Jewish scribes, who reverently preferred to copy an obscure text exactly rather than attempt to clarify it by an emendation. In this they were more modest, and more scientific, than many modern critics. In the hey-day of the criticism that reached its peak at the turn of the century, scholars were quick to infer that a passage which they could not understand must be corrupt. They then proceeded to 'correct' it. Some problems have been solved in this way, for even the Masoretic Text is not without its blemishes; but more often than not rewriting the text does not solve the problem. It merely destroys the evidence.[13]

Critical theories also assert that the prologue dates from an earlier period than that of the prose and epilogue section. But again, the evidence leans strongly against such subjective theories. In fact, ancient literature from the Near East has many examples of similar constructions which parallel the literary form of Job.[14] Furthermore, attempts are made to assert the disunity of Job as additional evidence for its dating and textual problems. Such reasoning fails to consider this: when Job is taken *in toto*, rather than in a fragmentary fashion, its unity is consistent and uniform. Job must be approached in an objective, bird's eye manner rather than a subjective, fragmentary manner.[15]

The Outline of Job: A Summary

Generally, the book of Job consists of poetry inserted between a brief introduction and conclusion. A more specific subdivision of Job reveals a fourfold breakdown of the forty-two chapters of Job.

In the prologue, Job and his character, background, and family are introduced. A challenge concerning Job's true devotion to God is then presented. Satan, asserting that Job serves God because of blessing rather than true devotion, is allowed by God to inflict Job with the loss of both his children and his physical health. Job, an innocent man, is thus afflicted with severe suffering for reasons unknown to him.

After Job's suffering is in progress, a thirty-four-chapter debate begins between Job and his three "friends," Eliphaz, Bildad, and Zophar. There was also a final speaker, Elihu. Concerning these four characters, Dr. John Frankland Genung, the late professor of literary and biblical interpretation, Amherst College, writes:

> The characters of the friends, while representing in general a remarkable uniformity of tenet, are quite aptly individualized: Eliphaz as a venerable and devout sage who, with his eminent penetrativeness of insight, combines a yearning compassion; Bildad more as a scholar versed in the derived lore of tradition; and Zophar more impetuous and dogmatic, with the dogmatist's vein of intolerance. In Elihu, the young Aramaean who speaks after the others, the writer seems endeavoring to portray a young man's positiveness and absoluteness of conviction, and with self-conceit that quite outruns his ability … [16]

Job, however, consistently appeals to his innocence before his friends and God. Job wins the debate, yet his suffering and lack of answers from God remain. In desperation, Job begs God for an answer. Then, just prior to God's response to Job, another friend, Elihu, attempts a final refutation of Job. Elihu fails.

Starting in chapter 38, God answers Job as to the whys of his suffering. Appealing to his absolute justice, power, wisdom, and sovereignty, God brings Job to a state of humble silence. Job is rendered speechless before the just yet personal God of the universe.

Concluding the book in chapter 42, Job concedes to the attributes of God as a satisfactory answer to his questions. Job then admits his utter ignorance of God's ways. Job repents in humility. God then asserts Job's innocence, and Job is fully restored and blessed of God.

The Justice of God in the Book of Job

To the Hebrew mind, the justice of God is of essential importance. If God is not just, then God is by definition not God. Concerning God's justice, Dr. Gordis writes that "the Book of Job demonstrates what could have been inferred a priori—a God without justice is not God to an ancient Hebrew."[17] Even Job echoes this cry for justice as he asks in Job 9:2 (NASB): "But how can a man be in the right before God?"

The nucleus of the problem of evil centers around God's justice. The very question of why an omnipotent, omniscient, sovereign, loving, and righteous God allows evil hinges on the reality and execution of His justice. Either God is just and other avenues of explanation for suffering are needed, or God is not just, which in effect renders any solution to the problem of evil as obsolete and futile. God is just or, by definition, He is not God.

A brief study of the Hebrew word for justice is valuable to understanding God's ways. The Hebrew word for justice or righteousness (*sedeq*) occurs 274 times in the Old Testament. This word "basically connotes conformity to an ethical or moral standard."[18] In addition, the earliest uses of this term are tied directly to judges and their duties. In this judicial context, these judges were to be both honest and impartial (Lev. 19:15).[19]

Of great significance is the find that *saddiq* is used to describe Job, himself. The late Dr. Harold G. Stigers, author and former professor and lecturer, states the following concerning this Hebrew word and its description of Job's character:

> The man who is righteous tries to preserve the peace and
> prosperity of the community by fulfilling the commands
> of God in regard to others. In the supreme sense the

righteous man (*saddiq*) is one who serves God. Specifically, he, like Job, delivers the poor and orphan, helps the blind along the way, supports the weak and is a father. This was the righteous "clothing" of Job's life. To return the poor man's pledged coat before sundown so that it may serve as his night clothes is righteousness (Deut 24:15), the purpose in this case being the man's comfort. But the "righteousness" consisted in obedience to God's law and conformity to God's nature, having mercy for the needy and helpless. Among other righteousness of Job were his care for the traveler (Job 31:31-32), eschewing wealth for its own sake (31:24-25), thus not victimizing himself or others in its pursuit. Nor did he squeeze out of his servants the last ounce of effort (31:13) having their limits of strength and comfort in mind. Job's long oath of innocence was a declaration of righteousness as the three friends recognized (32:1).[20]

Hence, the same root to describe God as just in the Old Testament is also used to describe Job. This leads to the conclusion that Job's suffering was not the result of retribution from God. Because God is just, and Job is righteous, other reasons are evident for Job's afflictions. The fact that God is just means this: God is always fair and will not render an unjust verdict on an undeserving person. No fact, premise, or conclusion will escape the fairness of God's judgments toward humans.

When applied to God, justice (sedeq) carries powerful implications. Dr. Stigers writes:

Sedeq is used attributively when applied to God himself as to his character. The lord is the just judge (II Chr 12:6; Ps 11:7; Jer 12:1; Lam 1:18) even to the utmost degree as the judge of all the earth (Deut 52:4; Ps 119:157; Isa 5:16). Therefore his standards, his judgments set out in his word are righteous (Ps 119:144, 160, 172). Being everlasting, they are the confidence of his people and will not fail. God's hate of sin and love of righteousness (Psa 45:7) express his essential righteousness. Therefore righteousness and judgement are the habitation ("foundation" NASB, HIV) of God's throne, i.e. they always characterize his actions (Ps 97:2).[21]

Misinterpretations of divine justice often ignore two essential premises. First, the omniscience of God, and second, the eternity of God (His eschatological perspective of history). Because God is omniscient, the entire disposal of facts needed to execute a fair verdict are available to God's mind. God thus knows all the relevant data and can interpret it with perfection. His justice is thus based on what He knows to be true and untrue regarding humankind. Any conclusion and judgment God reaches is either right or He is not God. Furthermore, because humans do not possess such knowledge, what they may think are unjust verdicts by God are unjust verdicts by humans because they do not know all the relevant data. Finite humanity is no match for the infinite God when it comes to matters of divine justice as it applies to the human realm.

God also views time from the basis of eternity. He thus sees the overall picture of where the trials of finite existence will culminate. From God's perspective, human history is heading in a specific direction for a specific purpose. Humans are in no position to prejudge God when the entire duration of history is not yet completed. The God of the Bible does indeed have solutions and plans for the complete elimination of evil and suffering, yet such solutions demand the patience of humans about the power of God.

The God of Job is not only just—He is the standard of justice. Yet, this justice is not a cold, judicial function of God, but instead God's justice is clothed and surrounded by His love, mercy, and goodness. The function of God's justice is not a separate office from His character. God's fairness works in unison with and not in opposition to His other attributes. A just God without His love and other attributes operating in a perfect balance would merely be a "divine myth-dictator"—not the personal God of the Bible.

Conclusion: Lessons and Applications from Job

What can we learn from the record of Job as seen in the pain, mystery, awe, and power that surrounds such a book? First, hindsight, from Job's perspective, is certainly more valuable than foresight. Had Job succumbed to the thinking of his wife and four friends, the epilogue would be far different. Yet Job held fast to the justice and omniscience of God's ways toward man. The result was the ultimate vindication of Job. Job's power over men rested in his patience in God. As Dr. Anderson states:

> Men seek an explanation of suffering in cause and effect. They look backwards for a connection between prior sin and present suffering. The Bible looks forwards in hope and seeks explanations, not so much in origins as in goals. The purpose of suffering is seen, not in its cause, but in its result. The Bible commends God's self-restraint. The outworkings of His justice through the long processes of history, which sometimes require spans of many centuries, are part of our existence in time. It is easier to see the hand of God in spectacular and immediate acts, and the sinner who is not instantly corrected is likely to despise God's delay in executing justice as a sign that He is indifferent or even absent. We have to be as patient as God Himself to see the end result, or to go on living in faith without seeing it. In due season we shall reap, if we do not faint.[22]

Second, Job teaches us that God's omniscience blended with His silence demands humility, awe, and respect from humans. Man must first acknowledge his rational limitations at comprehending man's "highest good" before he asserts God's eternal "blunders." Immanuel Kant was wise in noting that the ultimate in arrogance is to attempt to defend God, let alone assail Him. Dr. Julius Guttmann, in his work *Philosophies of Judaism*, makes this similar point as he writes:

> Not suffering in general, but rather the suffering of the righteous, causes us to doubt the justice of God and

becomes a stumbling block. The Book of Job especially reveals to what extent everything revolves about this one question. Job does not revolt against the magnitude of his suffering. He would resign himself to it, if only he knew its reason. He is driven to rebellion because he suffers without cause, and because he feels himself the victim of God's despotism. He finds peace once again when he regains his belief in the meaningfulness of God's acts.

Only the Book of Job seems to question this principle when, as its sole answer to the doubts raised by humanity, it points to the impenetrable majesty of God. In spite of some signs apparently pointing to Moslem and Calvinist doctrines of the absolute and sovereign superiority of the divine over all ethical criteria, this is hardly the real intent of the Book of Job. The problem of theodicy is not settled for Job by saying that God is above all ethical criteria, but rather by the recognition of God's utter incomprehensibility paradoxically becoming a ground for trust in the meaningfulness of his providence, a providence of love and justice which is no less meaningful for remaining impenetrable to human understanding. Thus, even where biblical religion seems to verge most on an irrational conception of the divine will, it never relinquishes the basic conviction of an essential meaningfulness. Even the intelligibility of the divine will is merely limited, not nullified, by our deficient human understanding.[23]

Third, Job also teaches us the difference between finite despair and eternal hope as seen in the consummation of human history. It is as if Job is a microcosm of the patterns of human history. Job, like Adam, first existed in a state of innocence. Yet, through temptation from an outside will, man, like Job, was subjected to extensive cycles of attempting to restore his innocence through his own efforts. When all seemed lost, restoration arrived. Granted, Job was innocent, unlike mankind, but a similar eschatological pattern does emerge. Evil must therefore exist, not as a logical contradiction, but instead in reference to historical consummation. At the conclusion of time, eternity will supply clear solutions to present questions concerning theodicy. Until time's conclusion, man must learn to respond to suffering in a manner identical to Job's obedience and example.

Fourth, the poetical overtones in Job supply a much-needed perspective on suffering. Only the poet can shed light on issues where the limitations of prose are evident. When poetry is blended with divine inspiration, a powerful communication tool is born. Dr. Emil G. Kraeling, the late assistant professor of Old Testament at Union Theological Seminary, comments on the poetry of Job:

> A Poetic work suggests more than it expresses; it strives to say a few things impressively rather than all things comprehensively. Hence we cannot expect to find it weighing all the conceivable pros and cons, like a book of philosophy.[24]

From the above, Kraeling moves to what must be our fifth lesson from Job. Job shows us that neither God's goodness nor His justice is at stake because He has a greater good in end.

> In short, the story is many-sided. It indicates that God, out of consideration for celestial beings, sometimes permits things to happen which are contrary to his love, in order that some desirable end may be attained. In this case it was a great end—to prove beyond a doubt that there is such a thing as an unselfish love of God among men.[25]

When Satan thus asked God in the prologue in Job 1:9 (NASB), "Does Job fear God for nothing?", the answer was in the proof of Job's ultimate surrender to the will of God. Job did indeed love God, not for His benefits, but instead for who He is.

Sixth, Job also teaches us about the humility of the will. How often, when we are subjected to suffering, do we respond in bitterness and rebellion rather than in humble acceptance and tolerance? Job may not have given us every reason for evil, but he did show us a response: submissive humility to a will that is wiser than our own. Dr. Herbert Pingarette, the late professor of philosophy at the University of California, Santa Barbra, writes concerning Job:

> What is central in the notion that we become wise through suffering is the truth that suffering is, as has been said earlier, the humbling of the will. To suffer is to be compelled to endure, undergo, and experience the humbled will, rather than to be able to act and to accomplish one's will.
>
> The wisdom taught by suffering is the wisdom learned in living, not in books; it is the experience of the finitude and fallibility of the personal will, and also, in the perspective of human mortality, of its ultimate impotence and defeat. The message of suffering is thus implicit in suffering itself; it is not a lesson only contingently associated with and conveyed through suffering. The experience gives wisdom when we see the fact for what it is, when we experience the humbled will and see at last the will as humble, inherently finite, and fallible, and when we accept this truth in our very bones and not merely in theory.[26]

And last, Job teaches us that there are not always simple, easy answers to the problem of evil. Out of sincerity and love, people often attempt to comfort the suffering with a pat "answer" or Bible verse. Such efforts are needed, but wise and patient understanding is also a must in such counseling. Often the greatest help one can give the sufferer is the patience and warmth of a listening ear. Ultimately, the best comfort will come from the Comforter Himself.

From the trials of Job, we must now turn to triumph of Christ. Only considering the life, suffering and death, resurrection, and second coming of Jesus Christ do the questions of Job and mankind concerning evil receive a complete answer.

NOTES

1   William Bode, *The Book of Job and the Solution of the Problem of Suffering It Offers* (Grand Rapids, MI: Eerdmans, 1914), p. 7.

2   Robert Gordis, *The Book of Job: Commentary, New Translation, and Special Studies* (New York: Jewish Theological Seminary of America, 1978), xi.

3   Gleason L. Archer, *A Survey of Old Testament Introduction* (Chicago: Moody, 1974), 454.

4   Elmer B. Smick, "Job," *The Zondervan Pictorial Encyclopedia of the Bible*, vol. 3, ed. Merrill C. Tenney (Grand Rapids, MI: Zondervan, 1975), 603.

5   Archer, *op. cit.*, 457.

6   *Ibid.*

7   *Ibid.*, 457-58.

8   *Ibid.*, 459.

9   Gleason L. Archer, *The Book of Job: God's Answer to the Problem of Undeserved Suffering* (Grand Rapids, MI: Baker Book House, 1982), 15.

10   *Ibid.*, 16.

11   *Ibid.*, 17.

12   Herbert Fingarette, "The Meaning of Law in the Book of Job," *Hastings Law Journal* 29, no. 6 (July 78): 1581, 1585.

13   Francis I. Andersen, *Job: An Introduction and Commentary* (Downers Grove, IL: InterVarsity, 1976), 16.

14   J. B. Pritchard, *Ancient Near Eastern Texts* (Princeton: Princeton University Press, 1969), 407-10.

15   See John Samuel Feinberg, "The Literary and Theological Implications of the Prologue and Epilogue of the Book of Job," Thesis, Talbot Theological Seminary, 1971, 1-42.

16   John Frankland Genung, "Job," *The International Standard Bible Encyclopedia*, vol. 3, eds. James Orr, John L. Nuelesen, and Edgar Y. Mullins (Grand Rapids, MI: Eerdmans, 1939), 1680.

17   Robert Gordis, *The Book of God and Man: A Study of Job* (Chicago: University of Chicago Press, 1965). 127.

18   Harold G. Stigers, "Sadeq," *Theological Wordbook of the Old Testament*, vol. 2, eds. R. Laird Harris, Gleason L. Archer, and Bruce K. Waltke (Chicago: Moody, 1980), 752.

19   *Ibid.*

20   *Ibid.*, 753.

21   *Ibid.*, 754.

22   Anderson, *Ibid.*, 68.

23   Julius Guttmann, *Philosophies of Judaism* (New York: Schocken Books, 1973), 17-18.

24   Emil G. Kraeling, *The Book of the Ways of God* (New York: Charles Scribner's Sons, 1937, 244.

25   *Ibid.*, p. 248.

26   Fingarette, *op. cit.*, 1604-5.

CHAPTER 4

Jesus Christ: His Suffering as a Redemptive Solution to Evil

Truly, Jesus Christ, the Christ of the Gospels, the Christ of history, the crucified and risen Christ, the divine-human Christ, is the most real, the most certain, the most blessed of all facts. And this fact is an ever-present and growing power which pervades the Church and conquers the world, and is its own best evidence, as the sun shining in the heavens. This fact is the only solution of the terrible mystery of sin and death, the only inspiration to a holy life of love to God and man, the only guide to happiness and peace. Systems of human wisdom will come and go, kingdoms and empires will rise and fall, but for all time to come Christ will remain "the Way, the Truth, and the Life [John 14:6 NKJV]."[1]

Of all the available options toward a solution to the problem of evil, biblical Christianity asserts the most stunning of them all: God became incarnate in Christ. By God becoming a man, not only was the bridge from eternity to time crossed, but God revealed His willingness to live, suffer, and die to supply a solution to the problem of evil. This means that God enacted a twofold solution: first, redemption, and second, glorification. God thus established his salvation in time and space as a basis for "a new heaven and a new earth" (Rev. 21:1 NIV). The suffering of Christ in time was the elimination of evil for humans in the future. Christ had to suffer so that humans may one day never suffer.

The analysis that follows will examine the reality that God Almighty did indeed suffer for man. Patripassianism is not a contradiction but a reality when the incarnation is interjected (the humanity of Christ). Hence, when the finished work of Christ through His redemption is applied, it is evident that God did not passively twiddle His omnipotent thumbs as evil ran its course but instead became directly involved through brutal suffering in the person of Christ. If sin is a dominant cause of evil and Christ died on the cross to eradicate sin, then Christ had a dominant effect on eliminating evil.

Our study will pursue a threefold analysis. First, a linguistic study of the predominant Greek word for suffering in the New Testament (*pascho*) will be examined. Second, a brief discussion of Christological doctrines that are relevant to evil and suffering will be analyzed. Third, a pointed study of the procedures and physical mutilation involved in Roman crucifixion will be discussed.

A Linguistic Survey of Suffering in the Scripture

Generally, scripture uses a wide variety of Hebrew and Greek terms to define and illustrate suffering.[2] To best serve our analysis, our focus must rest in the most frequent and important word for suffering in the New Testament: pascho.

In its classical usage, the exact derivation of pascho is uncertain, but starting with Homer and beyond, pascho means basically "'to experience something' which comes from without and which has to be suffered: 'something encounters me,' 'comes upon me,' 'to suffer evil.'"[3] Progressing to the Septuagint (the earliest Greek translation of the Old Testamant), usage of pascho, it is found twenty-one times with a Hebrew original existing in a mere five passages.[4] Pascho in the Old Testament was also valued for its educational purposes:

> The interpretation of suffering as a means of instruction is orientated, not anthropocentrically, ethically and philosophically, but soteriologically, religiously and theologically.[5]

The New Testament usage of pascho exposes the full impact of Christ's relevance to suffering. This term is used forty-two times in the NT with an especially important fact surrounding it: "Most of the refs [of *pascho*] are to the sufferings of Christ Himself and to the sufferings of Christians for His sake."[6] In the Gospels, pascho is used twelve times referring to the suffering of Christ (e.g., Lk. 9:22 NASB), "The Son of Man must suffer many things."). In Acts it is used four times; in Corinthians, Galatians, Philippians, Thessalonians, and 1 and 2 Timothy, pascho refers to believers suffering personally and for the sake of Christ. In Hebrews, Christ is proclaimed as the great high priest and mediator with pascho used four times to refer to Christ suffering. And in 1 Peter, pascho is used twelve times as a support for the major theme in 1 Peter, which develops a "theology of suffering."[7]

From the above evidence, the concept of suffering in the New Testament is predominantly correlated with the life, death, resurrection, and second coming of Christ. Such a close connection between Christ and suffering tells us that Christ was an integral part in a biblical solution to pain and evil. The usage of the term pascho presents us with a Christ who was both a partaker of and a solution to the suffering of humankind. One point is clear: Christ came to suffer (Acts 17:3).

The Incarnation and Suffering

By means of the incarnation, God did not sit passively by and allow evil and suffering to reign unchallenged. God became a man in Christ so that, in a human sense, God might suffer for man.[8] In the person of Christ, being fully God and fully man, God suffered for humans so that man may one day be free from suffering. Such a divine invasion reveals that God was willing to take the risk of directly involving Himself toward a solution to evil and suffering. Because of the incarnation and subsequent death of Christ on the cross, God must never be accused of a "limited" omniscience. In the incarnation, God boldly wore a suit of flesh so that humankind could receive rescue by the death of Christ. Hugh Evan Hopkins states:

> The cross spells out the love of God in a historic event. It is
> an emblem raised against every dark horizon to resist the

agnostic's denial. Take the cross away, and the darkness of suffering is suggestive of an indifferent God, who having created a world liable to run into trouble, seems to do nothing to help. But when Jesus was lifted up to die, what appeared to the sympathetic bystander as act of sheer cruelty and wicked injustice became the sign by which all men could read that God's love is undeniable.[9]

The meaning of the term incarnation is best represented by the apostle John's phrase asserting that "the Word became flesh, and dwelt among us."[10] Derived from the Latin term *incarnatio*, which means "taking or being flesh," this concept aptly sums up Christ as the "absolute immanence of God."[11] Referring to the above passage in John, Dr. Benjamin Breckinridge Warfield, the late professor of systematic theology at Princeton Theological Seminary, writes:

> "The Word" is a personal name of the eternal God; "flesh" is an appropriate designation of humanity in its entirety, with the implications of dependence and weakness. The meaning, then, is simply that He who had just been described as the eternal God became, by a voluntary act in time, a man. The language employed intimates merely that it was a definite act, and that it involved a change in the life-history of the eternal God, here designated "the Word." The whole emphasis falls on the nature of this change in His life-history. He became flesh. That is to say, He entered upon a mode of existence in which the experiences that belong to human beings would also be His. The dependence, the weakness, which constitute the very idea of flesh, in contrast with God, would now enter into His personal experience.[12]

Hence, Christ, although fully God,[13] was also fully man. He possessed a human body no different than any other man of His day. Not only did Christ possess a physical body that experienced the five senses, He also was a human being who thought, felt, laughed, and cried like any other individual. Christ was human in physical and psychological aspects of common human experience. He was God and man, yet without sin.

In addition to the clear biblical affirmations regarding the incarnation,[14] the earliest of the church fathers attested to the incarnation as fact. Polycarp, who was a disciple of the apostle John, writes in 155 AD: "Everyone who does not confess that Jesus Christ has come in the flesh is an Antichrist."[15] Ignatius, in 110 AD, states:

> There is one Physician, who is both flesh and spirit, born and not born, who is God in man, true life in death, both from Mary and from God, first able to suffer and then unable to suffer, Jesus Christ our lord.[16]

And Tertullian, in his classic "Apology," 197 AD asserts:

> Therefore, that Ray of God, as was ever foretold in the past, descended into a certain Virgin and was formed flesh in her womb, and was born God and man combined. The flesh, formed by the Spirit, is nourished, grows into manhood, speaks, teaches, acts, and is the Christ.[17]

Considering the preceding discussion, we must note that God cannot be indicted for not executing His omnipotence regarding evil. Only an omnipotent Creator could accomplish such an incarnational wonder. Furthermore, in a most intimate sense, God, through Christ's incarnation, identified with man. Because Christ is fully God and fully man, and He endured intense suffering as a man, can we not say (in a human sense) that God indeed suffered for man? The biblical theist can thus view evil and suffering from the standpoint of the God who has known both the divine sending and the human suffering of His very Son.

Redemption and Suffering

With the doctrine of redemption now the focus of our attention, one must always bear in mind that God paid an awesome price in His elimination of evil. For God to redeem man involved a great cost—the death of His own Son. Again, God was by no means passive. Man's redemption from evil meant that the blood of Christ had to be shed, for Hebrews 9:22 (NASB) states that "without shedding of blood there is no forgiveness."[18] Such a ransom on humans' behalf hardly reflects a God who is insensitive to evil and suffering. Warfield expresses this same point as he states:

> "Redeemer," however, is a title of more intimate revelation than either "lord" or "Savior." It gives expression not merely to our sense that we have received salvation from Him, but also to our appreciation of what it cost Him to procure this salvation for us. It is the name specifically of the Christ of the cross. Whenever we pronounce it, the cross is placarded before our eyes and our hearts are filled with loving remembrance not only that Christ has given us salvation, but that He paid a mighty price for it.[19]

At the heart of redemption is the concept of *ransom*, for redemption meant much more than just deliverance. The following definition explains exactly the full impact of redemption:

> Whenever men by their own fault or through some superior power have come under the control of someone else, and have lost their freedom to implement their will and decisions, and when their own resources are inadequate to deal with that other power, they can regain their freedom only by the intervention of a third party.[20]

The Greek term generally used for redemption in classical, Old Testament, and New Testament periods stemmed from the root word *lyo*, meaning "to loose." In its classical usage, *lopton* was often used referring to the freeing of prisoners of war and slaves, if the payment of a price was involved.[21] In its LXX usage, *lupton* referred to two concepts: family obligation and the paying of a price. Again, much like the classical usage, redemption was established through the payment of a price.[22]

In the New Testament, *lyo* is used forty-three times and means to loose, untie, set free, release, annul, or abolish. Its key derivative, *lupton*, is used only twice, yet these identical verses express the exact meaning of the ransom concept. Both Matthew 20:28 and Mark 10:45 (NASB) state that Christ was "to give his life a ransom for many."

This giving of Christ's life centered on the cross as the necessary means of redemption. The cross is essential to redemption for two main reasons. First, God demands the shedding of blood, as mentioned earlier, for forgiveness to ensue. Second, Christ's death was a vicarious and substitutionary death for the sin of humans.

Throughout the Old Testament, God demanded the shedding of blood as the only cleansing agent adequate to cover the sins of Israel. Blood, characteristic of its life-giving qualities, was used in the bulk of the Old Testament sacrificial ceremonies as the only life-symbol that would satisfy God and serve as a payment for sin. God's standard was clear: no blood, no forgiveness. Consequently, the shedding of Christ's blood on the cross was the ultimate and perfect act that met God's blood-standard for absolute forgiveness. For the full price of sin to be paid, the blood of Christ, which was shed on the cross, was God's absolute and essential requirement.

The cross was also necessary for redemption because of Christ's vicarious, substitutionary death. The sacrifice that God demanded for redemption had to possess two qualifications. First, it had to be connected to the bloodline of humankind to atone for human sin. Secondly, the sacrifice had to be perfect, without blemish. Hence, Jesus Christ was the only person eligible to die for humans. God's wrath could not be satisfied unless Christ died in the place of humankind.

The results of this death were that man was forgiven. The full penalty of sin was in a sense "transferred" from humankind to Christ as He suffered and died on the cross. Those who professed faith in Christ were eligible to receive the blessings and eternal inheritance that is included in salvation. Thus, true forgiveness involves a cost, which in God's case was the death of His very Son. Once the cross of Christ was finished, sin was finished. God *covered* the sin of humans with the blood of His Son so that never again would sin have dominion over man.

H. STUART ATKINS

Justification and Suffering

Central to the Christological solution to evil and suffering is the application of justification and regeneration. These two doctrines are logically connected in their application to faith in Christ. As the late Dr. Henry C. Theissen, professor of systematic theology at Dallas Theological Seminary, states: "In regeneration man receives a new life and a new nature; in justification, a new standing."[23] Justification then applies in a forensic framework while regeneration exhibits a transforming effect on the believer.

Regarding justification, the following is a superb definition of this doctrine by Dr. H. D. McDonald, the late vice principal and professor of historical theology and philosophy of religion at London Bible College:

> Justification is that judicial act of God's free mercy whereby He pronounces guiltless those sinners condemned under the law, constitutes them as actually righteous, once and for all, in the imputed righteousness of Christ—on the grounds of His atoning work, by grace, through faith alone apart from works—and assures them of a full pardon, acceptance in His sight, adoption as sons, and heirs of eternal life, and the present gift of the Holy Spirit; and such as are brought into this new relation and standing are by the power of this same Spirit, enabled to perform good works which God hath before ordained that we should walk therein. Yet, such works performed, as well as the faith out of which they spring, make no contribution to the soul's justification, but they are to be regarded as declarative evidences of a man's acceptance in the sight of God.[24]

Justification is thus a declaration by God that the one professing faith in Christ is righteous. In short, there is nothing one can do to add to the cross. The believer is declared righteous because God sees the blood of Christ rather than sin. Hence, the Greek term for righteousness, *dikaiosis*, is clearly understood to mean "justification, vindication, acquittal, to pronounce or treat as righteous."[25]

Ernst Achilles has aptly summarized the application of evil to justification and sanctification:

> The problem of evil is solved only by justification and sanctification. The one who has been justified is in the sphere of influence of the One who has conquered evil and gives the Spirit. Hence, he does not face the powers of evil without strength (Rom. 13:10; I Cor. 13:5; II Cor. 13:17).[26]

From our brief analysis above, we note that humans do not have to wait in fear regarding sin, evil, death, and life everlasting. We can know with confidence that Christ, not man, was responsible for securing a salvation far stronger than any pain or suffering. No matter what degree of suffering one must endure, the certainty that God declares the Christian as righteous is a sure comfort from any affliction.

Regeneration and Suffering

If any man or woman is a Christian, he is not just an "overhaul," but instead represents a "new creation."[27] Through faith in Christ, biblical theism promises a radical transformation of the innermost depths of human life and perception. This new creation is doctrinally called regeneration.

Regeneration is the complete transformation of an individual's old nature to that of a new nature. Through a supernatural act of God, an individual is changed from the state of a hopeless and lost sinner to that of a redeemed child of God. In essence, a regenerated person has gone from spiritual death to spiritual life.

The New Testament uses this term, *palingenesis*, only two times (Matt. 19:28; Titus 5:5). In its purest form, this word means "rebirth or regeneration." Thus, a radical change in the moral fiber of the inner man brings forth a metamorphosis of new life. Dr. John Nuelsen, the late bishop of the Methodist Episcopal Church, Zurich, Switzerland, writes:

> Regeneration implies not merely an addition of certain gifts or graces, a strengthening of certain innate good, qualities, but a radical change, which revolutionizes our whole being, contradicts and overcomes our old fallen nature, and places our spiritual center of gravity wholly outside of our own powers in the realm of God's causation.[28]

The proceeding doctrines do not guarantee that Christians will not face suffering, pain, and disaster. Yet, they do provide a basis that reassures the biblical theist of a source outside of himself or herself that ultimately has conquered any pain he or she may face. The word of Christ supplied a present hope and a future guarantee that pain and suffering are not far from extinction.

Crucifixion: Suffering and Death by Physical Mutilation

Although the beauty of Middle Age and Renaissance art is unquestionable, its depiction of the crucifixion of Christ often falls short as to accuracy. A bloody crown of thorns, a spear-pierced side, and a few cuts hardly depicts the actual mutilation of first-century Roman crucifixion. In fact, Christ's body was probably beaten beyond recognition. The brutal results of Christ's crucifixion reveal the extreme degree that Christ did indeed suffer. There are few parallels of pain and suffering in the ancient and modern world that compare to the brutality that was witnessed outside of Jerusalem in 33 AD

After a brief investigation of the historical evidence regarding crucifixion, the painful context of such torture becomes relevant to the problem of evil and suffering. For example, the late Dr. Martin Hengel, professor of New Testament theology and early Judaism at the University of Tubingen in Germany, supplies illuminating background regarding ancient crucifixion:

> For the men of the ancient world, Greeks, Romans, barbarians and Jews, the cross was not just a matter of indifference, just any kind of death. It was an utterly

offensive affair, 'obscene' in the original sense of the word. Crucifixion was a punishment in which the caprice and sadism of the executioners were given full rein.[29]

The ancient opinion alone is not enough to expose the grim brutality of Christ's crucifixion. A more detailed description from a medical standpoint is needed. For example, C. Truman Davis, MD, MS, provides a detailed study in *Arizona Medicine* concerning the physiological and anatomical evidence pertaining to Christ's Passion and crucifixion. First, Davis describes the initial phase of Christ's suffering: his sweating of blood in the Garden of Gethsemane. In medical terminology, such a condition is called hematidrosis. Davis writes:

> The physical passion of the Christ begins in Gethsemane. Of the many aspects of this initial suffering, I shall only discuss the one of physiological interest; the bloody sweat. It is interesting that the physician of the group, St. Luke, is the only one to mention this.
>
> Though very rare, the phenomenon of Hematidrosis, or bloody sweat, is well documented. Under great emotional stress, tiny capillaries in the sweat glands can break, thus mixing blood with sweat.[30]

The second physical aspect of the Passion and crucifixion is the scourging of Jesus. Davis, in detail, describes the severe brutality of Jesus's precrucifixion punishment:

> Then, as the blows continue, they cut deeper into the subcutaneous tissues, producing first an oozing of blood from the capillaries and veins of the skin, and finally spurting arterial bleeding from vessels in the underlying muscles. The small balls of lead first produce large, deep bruises which are broken open by subsequent blows.[31]

Third, the placement of the crown of thorns, in addition to subsequent brutality, is described. Davis asserts:

> They [the Roman centurions] still need a crown to make their travesty complete. A small bundle of flexible branches covered with long thorns (commonly used for firewood) are plaited into the shape of a crown and this is pressed into His scalp.[32]

Fourth, Davis describes the pain and slow suffering of crucifixion:

> The crucifixion begins. Hours of this limitless pain, cycles of twisting, joint-rending cramps, intermittent partial asphyxiation, searing pain as tissue is torn from His lacerated back as He moves up and down against the rough timber. Then another agony begins. A deep crushing pain deep in the chest as the pericardium slowly fills with serum and begins to compress the heart.[33]

The preceding medical information shows that Jesus faced one of the most brutal forms of human suffering. For God to thus be accused of indifference toward evil and suffering ignores the facts. Jesus endured pain and suffering so that humans may conquer their greatest enemy: death and sin. Jesus suffered as an innocent man, not a guilty criminal. He was crucified for who He claimed to be, not what He did. Yet the benefits of such innocent suffering had more effect on human nature and history than any other event. The very suffering of Christ resulted in a greater good because of the results of His death: redemption, justification, and regeneration for those who place their trust in His finished work.

Conclusion

Considering the preceding analysis, we have seen that Christ was not immune to the suffering of humankind. The New Testament is explicitly clear in making Christ a key focal point regarding suffering. In fact, without the suffering of Christ, there would be no Christianity, and thus no viable option open for a valid solution to evil and suffering. We must observe three applications concerning the problem of evil as it relates to Christ's work.

First, without redemption, the problem of evil would be unsolvable. God, however, has intimately involved Himself in history through the incarnation of Christ. God must never be indicted for a restraint of His omnipotence considering the miracles of the incarnation and the resurrection. The greatest result of suffering—death—was conquered through the resurrection of Christ.

Second, God's twofold plan for the elimination of evil and suffering—redemption and glorification—must always shape the framework of theodicy. The past, present, and future are no surprise to God's omniscience. The skeptic must not prejudge God's stage of history until all the acts are completed.

Third, Christ's ministry was often directed to those who faced vast suffering. His ministry of healing brought the elimination of great pain and discomfort to multitudes of individuals. Christ clearly had the power to bring healing and restoration to any affliction.

Fourth, God is not finished with history yet. The span of time present and future still awaits the second coming of Christ, where a new heavens and a new earth will be established. As Carl F. H. Henry writes:

> All the created universe awaits eschatological finalities
> that involve a new heavens and earth wholly free from
> suffering, sin and death, where the sovereign living God
> will be fully known as he is, the God who brings to glory
> and holy joy all those who put their faith in him.[34]

The final word must come from the most important passage in the New Testament concerning evil and suffering:

> He shall wipe away every tear from their eyes; and there
> shall no longer be any death; there shall no longer be any
> mourning, or crying, or pain.[35]

NOTES

1   Philip Schaff, *History of the Christian Church*, vol. 1 (Grand Rapids, MI: WM. B. Eerdmans, 1910), 111.

2   See H. L. E. Luering, "Suffering," *The International Standard Bible Encyclopedia*, vol. 4, ed. James Orr (Grand Rapids, MI: Wm. B. Eerdmans, 1939), 2869-70.

3   Wilhelm Michaelis, "pascho," *Theological Dictionary of the New Testament*, vol. 5, ed. Gerhard Friedrich Kittel, trans. & ed. Geoffrey W. Bromiley (Grand Rapids, MI: Wm. B. Eerdmans, 1967), 904.

4   *Ibid.*, 907.

5   *Ibid.*, 908.

6   *Ibid.*, 912.

7   See B. Van Elderen, "Peter, First Epistle," *The Zondervan Pictorial Encyclopedia of the Bible*, vol. 4, ed. Merrill C. Tenney (Grand Rapids, MI: Zondervan, 1975), 723-26.

8   See Kazoh Kitamori, *Theology of the Pain of God* (Richmond, VA: John Knox, 1965), 47, 114-15.

9   Hugh Alexander Evan Hopkins, *The Mystery of Suffering* (Chicago, IL : Inter-Varsity, 1959), 111.

10 John 1:14 (NASB).

11 V. W. Johnston, "Incarnation," *The Zondervan Pictorial Encyclopedia of the Bible*, vol. 3, ed. Merrill C. Tenney (Grand Rapids, MI: Zondervan, 1975), 271.

12 Benjamin B. Warfield, "Person of Christ," *The International Standard Bible Encyclopedia*, vol. 4, ed. James Orr (Grand Rapids, MI: Wm. B. Eerdmans, 1939), 2343.

13 See John Warwick Montgomery, "Jesus Christ And History, Part II: The Divinity of Jesus Christ," *Where Is History Going?* (Minneapolis, MN: Bethany House, 1972), 53-74.

14 Jn. 1:1-14; Rom. 1:2-5; 1 Tim. 3:16; Phil. 2:6-11.

15 Polycarp, "Letter to The Philippians," in *The Faith of the Early Fathers*, vol. 1, trans. W. A. Jurgens (Collegeville, MN: Liturgical Press, 1970), 29.

16 *Ibid.*, 18.

17 *Ibid.*, 114.

18 Heb. 9:22 (NASB).

19 Benjamin Breckinridge Warfield, *The Person and Work of Christ* (Grand Rapids, MI: Baker Book, 1950), 325.

20 Colin Brown, "Redemption," *The New International Dictionary of New Testament Theology*, vol. 3, ed. Colin Brown (Grand Rapids, MI: Zondervan, 1978), 177.

21   Leon Morris, *The Apostolic Preaching of the Cross* (Grand Rapids, MI: Wm. B. Eerdmans, 1955), 12-13.

22   *Ibid.*, 20.

23   Henry Clarence Thiessen, *Lectures in Systematic Theology* (Grand Rapids, MI: Wm. B. Eerdmans, 1949), 271.

24   H. D. Macdonald, "Justification by Faith," *Basic Christian Doctrines*, ed. Carl F. H. Henry (Grand Rapids, MI: Baker Book, 1962), 213-14.

25   See Brown, *op. cit.*, 352-77.

26   Ernst Achilles, "Evil," *The New International Dictionary of New Testament Theology*, vol. 1, ed. Colin Brown (Grand Rapids, MI: Baker Book, 1967), 564.

27   1 Cor. 5:17 (NASB).

28   John L. Nuelsen, "Regeneration," *The International Standard Bible Encyclopedia*, vol. 4, ed. James Orr (Grand Rapids, MI: Wm. B. Eerdmans, 1939), 2549.

29   Martin Hengel, *Crucifixion* (Philadelphia: Fortress, 1977), 22, 25.

30   C. Truman Davis, "The Crucifixion of Jesus: The Passion of Christ from a Medical Point of View," *Arizona Medicine* (March 1965):184.

31   *Ibid.*, 185.

32   *Ibid.*, 185-86.

33   *Ibid.*, 186-87.

34   Carl F. H. Henry, "Evil as a Religious Dilemma," *God, Revelation, and Authority*, 6 vols. (Waco, TX: Word Books, 1976-1983), 6:304.

35   Rev. 21:4 (NASB).

CHAPTER 5

Logic and the Problem of Evil

In its simplest form the problem is this: God is omnipotent; God is wholly good; and yet evil exists. There seems to be some contradiction between these three propositions, so that if any two of them were true the third would be false. But at the same time all three are essential parts of most theological positions; the theologian, it seems, at once must adhere and cannot consistently adhere to all three.[1]

With the application of logical thinking to theism, both turn out to be compatible bedfellows. However, the question remains: "Is theism consistent when the basic rules of logic are applied to one additional guest—the problem of evil?" In no other rational tool is the problem of evil exposed so effectively as in logic and critical thinking. From premise to conclusion, the issue becomes clear: God's very existence seems questionable considering the reality of unexplained, random evil. If God is good and loving, then why does evil exist? If God is all-powerful, why does He allow evil? These are but a few of the crucial questions surrounding evil.

In a brief attempt to vindicate the argument for the consistency of theism, we will state and critique the most common objections raised against theism. Before this, a list of logical terms and fallacies will be defined. Then we will present the moral argument concerning evil. Second, the argument from gratuitous (random) evil will be stated and analyzed. In the critique of both these arguments, an attempt will be made to consistently expose the fallacies inherent in these nontheistic arguments.

Ironically, in trying to expose fallacies, the nontheist has himself committed serious fallacies. Although these arguments appear valid in logical form, they are unsound in substance; hence, because of false premises, they pose no significant threat to the theism in a world where evil exists. Both the details and definitions matter.

Definition of Logical Terms

Before we state and criticize the formal arguments against theism, the precise meaning of the logical terms employed must be defined. This will be of help for both semantic reasons and for those unfamiliar with logical terminology. The following are the terms and their definitions:

1. Argument: A list of sentences (premises) offered in support of another sentence (the conclusion).[2]
2. Deductively valid argument: An argument such that if its premises are true, then its conclusion must be true. The premises of a valid deductive argument provide conclusive evidence for its conclusions.[3]
3. Inductively correct argument: An argument whose premises, if true, provide good but not necessarily conclusive evidence for its conclusion. An inductively correct argument may have true premises and a false conclusion.[4]
4. Sound argument: A deductively valid argument with true premises. All other deductively valid arguments are unsound.[5]
5. Ambiguity: The fallacy resulting from ambiguous use of terms. An ambiguous term is one that has more than one meaning.[6]
6. Begging the question: An argument that is viciously circular.[7]
7. Circular reasoning: Fallaciously using an intended conclusion, usually expressed in different words, to support that conclusion.[8]
8. Cogent argument: An argument that is valid, has warranted premises, and uses all relevant information available or known to the arguer.[9]
9. Fallacious argument: An argument that is not cogent, because it is invalid, has unwarranted premises, or fails to take account of available relevant information.[10]

10. Inconsistency: The fallacy of arguing from inconsistent premises or inconsistent conclusions. Also committed by an inconsistency between words and actions.[11]

11. Informal fallacy: A fallacy of content rather that structure.[12]

12. Questionable cause: The variety of the fallacy is a hasty conclusion in which we conclude (hastily) that one thing is the cause of something else.[13]

13. Extensional definition: A definition that lists all the things to which the word or phrase being defined applies.[14]

14. Ostensive definition: A definition that indicates the meaning of a word or phrase by pointing out a sample of the things denoted by the term.[15]

15. Stipulative definition: A definition that specifies, or stipulates, the meaning of a word or phrase.[16]

The Moral Argument against Theism

With the preceding definitions set forth, we now turn to the classic deductive argument concerning moral evil. It is this argument, first asserted by Epicurus, that best summarizes the supposed "contradictions" of theism. More currently, thinkers such as J. E. McTaggart,[17] C. J. Ducasse,[18] David Hume,[19] Anthony Flew,[20] J. Mackie,[21] John Stuart Mill,[22] H. D. Aiken,[23] and H. J. McCloskey[24] have proposed such arguments.

The following argument by Pierre Bayle (1647-1706) represents the classic argument against theism:[25]

1. Evil exists.
2. An omnipotent God could destroy evil.
3. A benevolent God would destroy evil.
4. Therefore, since evil is not destroyed, then either
   a. God is omnipotent and, hence, malevolent in some way, or
   b. God is benevolent and, hence, impotent in some way, or
   c. God is both malevolent and impotent, or
   d. There is no God at all.

Critique and Analysis of the Moral Argument against Theism

In our forthcoming critique of Bayle's argument, a point-by-point analysis of the premises and subpremises of his position will best serve our interest. Special attention will be given to the definitions of crucial words. For, in dealing with the problem of evil, the entire "issue over logical inconsistency rests on subtle and debatable interpretations of various Christian beliefs about the character of God, the meaning of evil, the nature of moral obligation, and a number of other matters."[26]

Although valid in its logical form, Bayle's argument, like that of many skeptics and nontheists, is unsound due to false and ill-defined premises. Validity does not always imply soundness. Bayle's argument is thus valid in *form*, but unsound in *content*. What appears to be a logical contradiction concerning evil and the existence of God is really a failure of Bayle to precisely define and understand his terms. Weak theology, poor semantics, and faulty reasoning possess the greatest threat to Bayle's thinking.

1. Evil exists.

The first premise of Bayle's argument leaves little room for error or doubt. The real world shows clear evidence of the reality of evil. Just a quick glance at the daily newspaper confirms that evil (in its moral and gratuitous form) is everywhere. In fact, to deny evil (illusionism) is itself an illusion. This premise thus must be granted as true because it fits the facts and experience of life.

2. An omnipotent God could destroy evil.

In this next premise, the importance of precise semantics arises. Two words must be defined: "omnipotent" and "destroy." When one states that God is "omnipotent," in basic terms this means that God is all-powerful. However, this does not mean "that there are no limits to God's power, but at most that there are no nonlogical limits to what He can do."[27]

God does not play omnipotent games with the universe by creating square circles, unmarried bachelors, or rocks too heavy for Him to lift.

Such "puzzles" are illogical absurdities. God's power is ultimate, absolute, and not limited in any manner, except for reasons that His love, wisdom, knowledge, justice, and omniscience would restrain for purposes that would result in a greater good (i.e., a nondeterministic world in which free will is exercised). Hence, God is *able* but not *willing*. Dr. Addison H. Leitch illustrates this point lucidly:

> The question as to how sin entered into the world is not a question of His omnipotence as much as it is a means of illustrating how an all-powerful God can create a system in which sin is possible and at the same time, because of His omnipotence, make the wrath of man to serve Him.
>
> The power of God implies the power of self-limitation. God suffers no internal or external compulsion. One cannot hold that He exercises all of His power all the time and in every place. God has power over His power which is always under His wise and holy will. It may never be said that He is a slave of His own omnipotence: men live in a personal not a deterministic system, and therefore they have freedom to act as individuals because He has restraint. God's omnipotence is in no sense a pantheistic attribute; omnipotence is not automatic but willful.[28]

In premise 2, Bayle states that an "omnipotent God could destroy evil," which implies, and is confirmed in premise 4 that He has not destroyed evil. Omnipotence thus seems to imply an all-powerful God who always executes His power in a full-scale capacity. However, as Leitch so clearly noted, God's omnipotence is a factor, yet it is not a flood that drowns out free will. Because God is all-powerful, God has the power to control His power. "All-powerful" thus means all-control. From the start, thus, it seems Bayle has adopted the fallacy of ambiguity.

Consequently, the term *destroy* is clouded with ambiguity and vagueness. Just what is meant by *destroy*? Various options may include a permanent, present, future, lack of, or a complete destruction of evil. Yet no attempt is included to supply a *stipulative* and *ostensive* definition of *destroy*. A mere definition is insufficient.

Concerning the word *destroy*, Dr, Norman Geisler writes:

> Does it mean to annihilate? If it means to annihilate, we should recall that it would be impossible to destroy evil that has occurred without also doing away with the moral universe and free choice. If "destroy" however, means to defeat, conquer, or make null and void, then it is possible that this is presently occurring.[29]

If this term does mean "to defeat" or "to conquer," then the assertions of biblical theism fit perfectly into Bayle's semantical void. Redemption, plus the coming of a new heavens and a new earth, provides future verification that God will indeed embark on a progressive and final plan for the destruction of evil.[30] Dr. Geisler further states:

> Bayle's argument has an arbitrary time limit on it. It says in effect that since God has not defeated evil until now, He never will.[31] An obvious response to this objection is to recognize that God may yet destroy evil in the future.[32]

Again, Bayle commits the fallacy of ambiguity.

3. A benevolent God would destroy evil.

Bayle assumes that benevolence implies destruction. If God is good, then He must never allow evil. Philo, in Hume's *Dialogues Concerning Natural Religion*, also asserts this point.[33] However, does divine goodness demand such a conclusion?[34] Hardly, for if there is a moral justification for God allowing evil, then He must not be prematurely indicted. Dr. Nelson Pike, with the agreement of the noted logician Alvin Plantinga,[35] argues:

> I do not think it follows from the claim that a being is perfectly good that he would prevent suffering if he could.

Consider this case. A parent forces a child to take a spoonful of bitter medicine. The parent thus brings about an instance of discomfort, suffering. The parent could have refrained from administering the medicine; and he knew that the child would suffer discomfort if he did administer it. Yet, when we are assured that the parent acted in the interest of the child's health and happiness, the fact that he knowingly caused discomfort is not sufficient to remove the parent from the class of perfectly good beings. If the parent fails to fit into this class, it is not because he caused this instance of suffering.

Given only that the parent knowingly caused an instance of discomfort, we are tempted to blame him for his action—that is, to exclude him from the class of perfectly good beings. But when the full circumstances are known, blame becomes inappropriate. In this case, there is what I shall call a "morally sufficient reason" for the parent's action. To say that there is a morally sufficient reason for his action is simply to say that there is a circumstance or condition which, when known, renders blame (though, of course, not responsibility) for the action inappropriate. As a general statement, a being who permits (or brings about) an instance of suffering might be perfectly good providing only that there is a morally sufficient reason for his action. Thus, it does not follow from the claim that God is perfectly good that he would prevent suffering if he could. God might fail to prevent suffering, or himself bring about suffering, while remaining perfectly good. It is required only that there be a morally sufficient reason for his action.[36]

To apply Pike's thinking, the "morally sufficient reason" rests in God's respect for man's free will. God may allow certain evils for the purpose of permitting necessary goods (i.e., the exercise of free will to choose good or evil). In this case, God's "spoonful of bitter medicine" was a dose of free will which allowed man the nondeterministic choice of good or evil.

Commenting on Wesley's position of God's goodness, the Rev. Jerry Walls states in *The Christian Scholars Review*:

> A good God is not indifferent to human suffering. He would not permit all the misery in this world unless there were some reason why he cannot prevent it. God is opposed to sin and its attendant misery. But since he has granted man freedom, he cannot eliminate all evil.
>
> It is important to stress that this is a logical point about the nature of freedom. That is, God's inability to eliminate all evil is not a weakness within himself. It is a logical consequence of his granting man freedom and of men using that freedom to choose evil.[37]

If these scholars are correct, divine goodness does not imply an inconsistency. Good does not imply would. Theism can still retain its consistency if the nontheist avoids the fallacy of ambiguity through ostensive and stipulative definitions. Again, an apparent logical problem lies more with Bayle's ambiguity than theism's "inconsistency."

4. Therefore, since evil is not destroyed, then either—

It is here, in Bayle's conclusion that the seeds of his fallacies in premises 1, 2, and 3 expand into additional fallacies. Not only does Bayle again employ the ambiguous term *destroy*, but he also begs the question and succumbs to the fallacy of questionable cause.

Bayle begs the question by choosing premises to which the theist is not committed. The theist is not committed to Bayle's use of "omnipotence" or "benevolence." The theist is not committed to his use of the term *destroy*. Nor is the theist committed to Bayle's assertion that "evil is not destroyed." Furthermore, the theist does assert that "God is destroying evil and will one day complete the process."[38] Granted, this answer still challenges the theist to answer why God permits evil and what verifiable reasons we have for its future elimination. Such a hasty conclusion on Bayle's part is presumption.

Furthermore, Bayle fails to utilize an essential element in theism's response to evil: free will. Although we have earlier discussed free will, it is paramount that we apply it again for further clarification. As free will is analyzed, it then becomes clear why evil is not destroyed at present.

First, because God is simultaneously aware of the past, present, and future, time as a finite dimension does not limit His ability to destroy evil. God knows the volitional choices of future actions, but He does not force a correct action. The crux of the matter seems to rest in the distinction between future knowledge and forceful determinism. Dr. Geisler asserts:

> It is fully possible that an eternal God may simply observe in His one eternal now what the murderer is freely doing, without determining what he does. Free choice does not mean that one will do otherwise. It only allows that one can do otherwise. God could know what the murderer will do without determining that the murderer must do it.[39]

Second, why did God not just create a world where men had free choice, yet they always choose the good? Dr. J. L. Mackie states this issue clearly:

> If God has made men such that in their free choices they sometimes prefer what is good and sometimes what is evil, why could he not have made men such that they always freely choose the good?[40]

To answer Mackie, one must make a distinction between possible worlds and actual worlds. [41] What is possible and what is actual are two different categories. The actual is what is real. The possible represents what could be. The actual is reality; the possible is conditional. Anything is possible, but not everything is actual. Geisler again notes:

> Not everything that is logically possible actually happens.
> My nonexistence is logically possible, but is not actually
> the case, since I do exist.[42]

Hence, it is possible a world could exist where volition is always good, yet the actual world is not so. Because of man's free will, God did not allow such a condition.

And third, causality sheds additional light on the application of free will to evil. Augustine has a superb definition of free will as it relates to causality:

> What cause of willing can there be which is prior to
> willing? Either will is itself the first cause of sin, or the
> first cause [i.e., a free creature] is without sin.[43]

Dr. Geisler paraphrases Augustine's thinking as he states:

> Free choice means self-caused actions. No action is
> uncaused, and actions caused by another are determined
> (i.e. not free). Hence, free actions are self-caused.[44]

Thus, for God to create a world where His creatures always choose good, by definition such a world would not be free; rather, it would be a determined world because man's continual choice of good would be caused or corrected by God. The cause of man's choices cannot regress beyond his own will,[45] thus man's choices are man's responsibility, not God's. The "unmoved mover" of human will is humankind's will.

Dr. John Warwick Montgomery asserts the importance of this preceding point:

> Opponents of theism have perennially argued that the
> natural and moral evils in the universe make the idea
> of an omnipotent and perfectly good God irrational.
> But if subjectivity (and its correlative, free will) must be
> presupposed on the level of human action, and if God's
> character as fully transcendent divine Subject serves to

make human volition meaningful, then the existence of freewill in itself provides a legitimate explanation of evil. To create personalities without genuine freewill would not have been to create persons at all; and freewill means the genuine possibility of wrong decision, i.e. the creation of evil by God's creatures (whether wide ranging natural and moral evil by fallen angels or limited chaos on earth by fallen mankind). As for the argument that a good God should have created only those beings he would foresee as choosing the right—or that he should certainly eliminate the effects of his creatures' evil decisions, the obvious answer is … that this would be tantamount to not giving freewill at all. To create only those who "must" (in any sense) choose good is to create automata; and to whisk away evil effects as they are produced is to whisk away evil itself, for an act and its consequences are bound together.[46]

a. God is omnipotent and, hence, malevolent in some way, or

In this first subconclusion of Bayle, God is placed in a framework of sadism. In short, God enjoys inflicting evil and suffering upon mankind. Rather than "reducing" or "modifying" His omnipotence, God becomes a merciless, unconcerned monster of sadistic terror. However, a sadistic God is not a tenet of theism. But why?

First, could not this sadistic god just be a finite demon or devil? If God is limited in love, He must also be limited in His moral nature, yet by what absolute reference point would one determine this? One could not say God was imperfect unless there was a standard beyond God. Thus, the ultimate reference point could be the God of biblical theism.[47]

Second, the actions of a sadistic God would cancel one another out in chaotic incompatibility. Such a God would construct and destroy the world at simultaneous moments. The world would be a love/hate machine occurring at the same time.[48]

b. God is benevolent, hence, impotent in some way, or

This second subconclusion, endorsed by thinkers such as William James, John Stuart Mill, and E. S. Brightman represents a prominent view of both nontheists and process theologians: theistic finitism. Since God is all-loving, yet has not eliminated evil, He must possess limited omnipotence. God is willing but not able.

However, this position is questionable for two reasons.[49] First, a God who is limited in power seems to be a creature rather than a creator. Only a "finite" god could fit such an antiomnipotent identity. As Dr. Geisler states:

> How can God be finite when every finite being must be caused? Wouldn't a finite God be no more than a giant creature in need of a Creator to explain its existence?[50]

If God is finite, who created Him? Because of contingency, would there not have to exist a cause independent of God that would explain His finitude? Furthermore, why would God "create a world in the first place if He knew He could not control the evil in it?"[51]

Second, what are the signs that show good is overcoming evil? Moral consistency in history seems brief. Short gains are evident, but ethically devastating reminders such as war and crime are quick to quiet moral optimism. Consequently, if God is finite, there is no assurance of God overcoming evil. Indeed, could such a finite God stop evil from overcoming good? If finite, He could not stop such chaotic and unpredictable dualism.

At best, finitism can encourage social action and present a more "human" understanding of God. A finite God is a compromise, rather a constructive attempt to reconcile God and evil. Theistic finitism clearly represents "the current fashion of facing the problem of evil by surrender of the attributes of absoluteness in the Deity."[52] Furthermore, theistic finitism pontificates, but never answers the question: "Is God finite?" Similar to having your cake and eating it, too, finitism worships their god yet limits Him.

d. There is no God at all.

Because subconclusion c is a culmination of a and b, further critique of this conclusion is fruitless. This does, however, bring us to Bayle's conclusion (i.e., that God may not exist). Such a conclusion is merely the result of a series of false premises that also render his conclusion false. As Dr. Kahane, professor of logic at the University of Maryland, states:

> Valid arguments that contain only true premises (and thus also have a true conclusion) are said to be sound arguments. Invalid arguments and valid arguments containing at least one false premise are said to be unsound arguments.[53]

Bayle's argument is thus valid but unsound due to his false premises. Validity indicates correct logical form, yet it does not, in the context of Bayle's argument, lead to his atheistic conclusion. Only a sound argument would pose a threat to theism, yet Bayle has failed to supply such an argument. Bayle's argument, and others like it, fail in logical precision and in the ability to see the following options:

> For several reasons, most nontheists have not pressed the argument [moral argument] as a definitive disproof. (1) First, it is possible that God is doing something to destroy evil. (2) Second, it is possible that there is some greater good in permitting evil. (3) Or, it is possible that what seems to be evil is part of a larger picture of good. (4) Fourth, it is possible that it would be in some way contradictory to God's nature to destroy evil, and even an omnipotent being cannot do the contradictory.[54]

The Gratuitous Argument against Theism

An analysis of the moral argument against theism is not enough. Consequently, the question of gratuitous evil (innocent suffering) remains and must be briefly addressed and summarized. The critical question is this: "Why do innocent people (i.e., children) suffer from sickness, tragic circumstances, or natural disasters such as earthquakes, floods, etc. for no apparent reason?" In a simplified form, the argument is as follows:

"An all-loving, all-powerful God would not allow innocent suffering.
There is innocent suffering in the world.
Therefore, there is not an all-loving, all-powerful God."[55]

To further analyze this argument, we must turn to a specific discussion of gratuitous evil by Dr. Michael Peterson, who proposes the following syllogism:

"(G) An omnipotent, omniscient, wholly good God exists."

In evaluating this claim, at least one auxiliary assumption is made. Many writers on the problem of gratuitous evil believe that God is utterly fastidious in preventing all evils from being gratuitous. This assumption may be labeled the principle of meticulous providence, and may be expressed thus:

(MP) "An omnipotent, omniscient, wholly good God would prevent or eliminate the existence of really gratuitous or pointless evils."

This principle, together with (G), implies that the proposition
(E-3) "Gratuitous or pointless evil exists,"

is false; that is, (E-3) is true. But in fact (E-3) appears to be true. This is the heart of the problem. The evidential argument from gratuitous evil can be condensed into the following model:

1.   If (G) is true, then, if (MP) is true, (E-3) should be true (theological premise).
2.   It is probable that (E-3) is true (factual premise).
3.   Therefore, it is probable that (G) is false (logical conclusion).[56]

Concerning this preceding argument, theism must provide an adequate solution, or gratuitous evil does indeed render theism inconsistent. To this task we now briefly turn.

Critique of the Gratuitous Argument against Theism

Peterson's important thrust is that gratuitous evil is logically linked to free will. He writes:

> If the conception of human free will is taken to involve the possibility of bringing about really gratuitous evil (specifically, moral evil), then God cannot completely prevent or eliminate gratuitous evil without severely diminishing free will. That would be logically impossible.[57]

Peterson seems to be saying that gratuitous evil is acceptable because of free will. If God were to remove gratuitous evil, He would also have to remove free will. The key concept Peterson uses is possibility, for if gratuitous evil is possible in relation to free will, such evil does not threaten the consistency of theism. Geisler writes:

> We must note that it is possible, in fact very probable, that suffering of some type will occur in a world where there are morally free agents. People sometimes exercise their freedom in such a way as to bring suffering to themselves or others either directly or indirectly.[58]

For God to eliminate gratuitous evil, He would be forced into a deterministic world. Only a free person has the option of choosing either good or evil. And if there is, by definition, no cause prior to willing (as Augustine noted), then free will cannot be determined. Thus, God could justify gratuitous evil in respect and protection of human freedom. Subsequently, this leads us to an additional point.

Natural Law and Gratuitous Evil

A second consideration of gratuitous evil involves natural law. The question arises: "Why so many pointless deaths from natural disasters?" If these disasters include the natural world, why does not God consistently intervene with miracles to stop such tragedies? Again, we cite Peterson:

> For God to eliminate the possibility of gratuitous natural
> evils arising from nonhuman causes is to eliminate a
> natural order altogether. But a natural order is required
> for the exercise of free will, as well as for a host of other
> things.[59]

Peterson's point is strong: because free will and the natural order operate on interconnecting and similar principles, to tamper with one would cause chaos in the other. For example, imagine what the world would be like if God intervened in every potential occurrence of innocent suffering. Bullets would turn to rubber, knives would melt, falling items would stop in midair, water would turn to ice just prior to an infant falling into an unattended pool, and a series of additional "altercations" of the natural order would occur. In short, the natural world would turn into a chaotic mess of divine intervention, which in turn would render the regularity of physical laws untrustworthy. If God is to violate free will, He must also violate natural law. Gratuitous evil can exist if the natural order is to remain functional, and if free will is to stay just that—free. Hence, meticulous providence (MP) is not a substantial refutation of gratuitous evil.

This in turn leads us to a revision of our first syllogism. Dr. Peterson revised the syllogism as follows:

> (PG) An omnipotent, omniscient, wholly good God could
> allow gratuitous or pointless evil.

1.   If (G) is true, then, assuming that (PG) is true, (E-3) could be true. (revised theological premise)
2.   *It is probable that (E-3) is true. (factual premise)*[60]

Summarizing the above argument, Peterson states:

> This argument turns on the belief that theism implies
> that gratuitous evil is at least possible in a theistic world.
> Since there are good reasons to think that gratuitous evil
> is actual, then it is obviously possible.[61]

As Peterson has argued, it is possible that God could allow gratuitous evil. With an understanding of free will and the natural order, the actualities of evil are reconcilable because of the attributes of God in reference to human freedom. The *possibility* of gratuitous evil implies the *plausibility* of gratuitous evil.

Conclusion

After our brief study of the preceding arguments against theism, one must demand the following from nontheists attempting to locate logical shortcomings in theism.

First, any acceptable approach to a logical examination of evil must include precise logic. More inconsistencies arose from the nontheistic methodology rather than from the theistic arguments in question.

Second, if one is to use logic as a tool for exposing the alleged inconsistencies of theism, the game must be played by correct logical rules. Ambiguity, circular reasoning, questionable cause, and other fallacies are serious problems in the nontheistic critique of the problem of evil.

Third, when any attribute of God is discussed, it must never be used in seclusion from His other attributes. For example, to say "God is love" does not define God. Rather, it is to speak of one aspect of God's character, an aspect which must be considered in relation to His other attributes. There is no room for superficial theology.

Fourth, the theist must demand soundness rather than just validity concerning arguments against theism.[62] The nature of the false premises that shape the thinking of many nontheists is clear evidence of validity without soundness.

Fifth, it is essential that evil be taken in the context of chapters 1 through 4 of our study. These chapters are an essential foundation for the logical and theological elements of the present discussion.

And last, logic alone is by no means the final answer to the problem of evil and suffering. A sound syllogism will not dry the tears of a woman mourning the death of her innocent child. At best logic can show us that there are theoretical and conceptual answers to apparent contradictions.

We must now shift to both the intellectual and experiential aspects of evil and suffering. Our final chapter will focus on the greatest apologist of the twentieth century: C. S. Lewis. In Lewis, we find a personified illustration and summation of the crucial issues in the preceding five chapters. Lewis not only thought deeply concerning the ramifications of pain and suffering; he also experienced firsthand the grief of observed pain. It is to this comfort from Narnia that we now turn.

NOTES

1   H. L. Mackie, "Evil and Omnipotence," *Mind* 64 (1955): 200.

2   Howard Kahane, *Logic and Philosophy: A Modern Introduction* (Belmont, CA: Wadsworth, 1982), 9.

3   *Ibid.*

4   *Ibid.*

5   *Ibid.*

6   *Ibid.*, 233.

7   *Ibid.*

8   *Ibid.*

9   *Ibid.*

10   *Ibid.*

11   *Ibid.*

12   *Ibid.*

13   *Ibid.*

14   *Ibid.*, 247.

15   *Ibid.*, 248.

16   *Ibid.*

17   J. E. Mctaggart, *Some Dogmas of Religion* (London, 1906), 212-13, cited in John Donnelly, *Logical Analysis and Contemporary Theism* (New York: Fordham University Press, 1972), 160.

18   C. J. Ducasse, *A Philosophical Scrutiny of Religion* (New York, 1953), Ch. 16, cited in *Ibid*.

19   David Hume, *Dialogues Concerning Natural Religion*, *The Hafner Library of Classics*, vol. 5, H. D. Aiken ed. (New York, 1955), 61-81, cited in *Ibid*.

20   Flew and MacIntyre eds., "Theology and Falsification," *New Essays in Philosophical Theology* (New York, 1955), 108, cited in *Ibid*.

21   J. L. Mackie, "Evil and Omnipotence," *Mind* 64 (1955): 201, cited in *Ibid*.

22   John Stuart Mill, *Theism*, (New York, 1957), 40. See also *The Utility of Religion* (New York, 1957), 73ff, cited in *Ibid*.

23   H. D. Aiken, "God and Evil: Some Relations between Faith and Morals," *Ethics* 68 (1958): 77-97, cited in *Ibid*.

24   H. J. McCloskey, "God and Evil," *Philosophical Quarterly* 10 (1960): 96-114, cited in *Ibid*.

25   Cited in Norman L. Geisler, *Philosophy of Religion* (Grand Rapids, MI: Zondervan, 1974), 125126. This is not an attempt to rely on a secondary source for Bayle's argument. For purposes of clarity, Geisler's summary of this argument is used. To verify the accuracy of Bayle's argument, see E. Beller

and M. Lee, eds. *Selections from Bayle's Dictionary* (Princeton, NJ: Princeton University Press, 1952), 157-83.

26   Michael Peterson, *Evil and the Christian God* (Grand Rapids, MI: Baker Book, 1982), 46-47.

27   Alvin C. Plantinga, *God, Freedom, and Evil* (Grand Rapids, MI: W. B. Eerdmans, 1974), 18.

28   A.H. Leitch, "Omnipotence," *The Zondervan Pictorial Encyclopedia of the Bible*, vol. 4, ed. Merrill C. Tenney (Grand Rapids, MI: Zondervan, 1975), 530.

29   Norman L. Geisler, *The Roots of Evil* (Grand Rapids, MI: Zondervan, 1978), 35.

30   See John Warwick Montgomery, *The Shape of the Past (*Minneapolis, MN: Bethany House, 1975), 114-79; John Warwick Montgomery, *Where Is History Going* (Minneapolis, MN: Bethany House, 1969).

31   Dr. Geisler footnotes this point as follows on page 92 of his work *The Roots of Evil*: "John Hick has argued that a position is at least meaningful to hold if one can specify the conditions in the future under which it can be verified." John Hick, "Theology and Verification," *The Existence of God* (New York: Macmillan, 1964), 252-54.

32   Geisler, *loc. cit.*

33   David Hume, *Dialogues Concerning Natural Religion*, ed. Henry D. Aiken (New York: Hafner, 1948), 61-81.

34   For a detailed analysis of God's goodness, see: John W. Wenham, *The Goodness of God* (Downers Grove, IL: InterVarsity, 1974).

35   Alvin Plantinga, *God and Other Minds* (Ithaca, NY: Cornell University Press, 1967), 124.

36   Nelson Pike, "Hume on Evil," *Logical Analysis and Contemporary Theism*, ed. John Donnelly (New York: Fordham University Press, 1972), 145-46.

37   Jerry L. Walls, "The Free Will Defense, Calvinism, Wesley, and the Goodness of God," *Christian Scholars Review* 8 (1983): 28.

38   Geisler, *op. cit.*, [in note 25 above], 350.

39   Geisler. *op. cit.*, [in note 29 above], 31*

40   J. L. Mackie, "Evil and Omnipotence," *Mind* 64 (1955): 209.

41   See Alvin Plantinga, *The Nature of Necessity* (New York: Oxford University, 1974), 164-95.

42   Geisler, *op. cit.*, 57-58.

43   Augustine, *On Free Will*, I, 1, 1; III, xvii, cited in Norman L. Geisler, *The Roots of Evil* (Grand Rapids, MI, 1978), 48-49.

44   Geisler, *op. cit.*, 50.

45   In an additional work, Geisler supplies important clarification on the issue of free will: "God causes man *metaphysically* but man causes himself *morally*. God is responsible for our *essence* but we are responsible for our free *actions*. God gave man the *fact* of freedom; man is responsible for the *acts* of freedom." Geisler

states further: "The essence of my own view is that (a) God *determines* all human actions by his knowledge of what men will freely do, not by his power to force them to do what he wants them to do, and (b) God is the *ultimate* cause of all free actions in that he gave us the power of choice, but we are the *immediate* cause of these free actions [Norman L. Geisler, "Man's destiny: free or forced?," *Christian Scholars Review* 9, no. 2 (1979): 108, 119.] Hence, responsibility for evil correlates to action (man's choices), rather than essence (God's creation). God is responsible for man's created essence, which includes the will, yet He is not responsible for the actions of that will. The ultimate cause of evil relates to divine creation; the immediate cause of evil relates to human volition. Ultimate cause, thus, does not imply immediate responsibility.

46   John Warwick Montgomery, "Is Man His Own God?" *The Suicide of Christian Theology* (Minneapolis, MN: Bethany Fellowship, 1970), 259.

47   *Ibid.*, 29.

48   *Ibid.*

49   For a critique of finitism, see Keith Yandell, "The Problem of Evil," paper presented for the Wheaton Annual Philosophy Conference, October 1980, cited in Michael Peterson, *Evil and the Christian God* (Grand Rapids, MI, 1982), 96.

50   *Ibid.*, 27.

51   Geisler, *op. cit.*, 26-27.

52   R. King, *The Problem of Evil* (New York: Ronald Press, 1952), 54.

53   Kahane, *op. cit.*, 8.

54   Geisler, *op. cit.*, [in note 25 above], 126.

55   Geisler, *op. cit.*, [in note 29 above), 35.

56   Peterson, *op. cit.*, 76-77.

57   Peterson, *op. cit.*, [in note 26 above], 104-6.

58   Geisler, *op. cit.*, 36.

59   *Ibid.*

60   *Ibid.*, 132.

61   Peterson, *op. cit.*, 132.

62   Concerning soundness, it is important to consider the following point of Dr. Kahane: "In general, logic is not concerned with the soundness of arguments, because with one exception, logic alone cannot determine whether the premises of an argument are true or false." [Kahane, *op. cit.*, 8.] The key term here is the word *alone*. Because logic in its content, but not in its formal sense, is lacking, correctives from theology and philosophy are essential to test and clarify the accuracy of premises involving theodicy.

CHAPTER 6

Comfort from Narnia: C. S. Lewis and the Problem of Evil

> Talk to me about the truth of religion and I'll listen
> gladly. Talk to me about the duty of religion and I'll
> listen submissively. But don't come talking to me about
> the consolations of religion or I shall suspect that you
> don't understand.[1]

Among the hundreds of bibliographies suggesting books concerning the problem of suffering, evil, and pain, there is one author who stands as a pillar of authority: C. S. Lewis. Wherever one looks, the name of Lewis and the titles of his two classic works, *The Problem of Pain* and *A Grief Observed*, carry international respect. In fact, it may be safe to say that any bibliography on suffering and pain without the name of Lewis is without the name of scholarship.

Our final chapter brings us to the finest defender of the Christian faith in the twentieth century: C. S. Lewis. Our task will not only include his works, but also his personal experience as he responded to both the intellectual and emotional facets of pain and suffering. Treatments of Lewis's writings on pain are often incomplete because they only include half the story—the intellectual as seen in his book *The Problem of Pain*— rather than also including the experiential as seen in his later book, *A Grief Observed*. A synthesis of both these works is essential to understand the full impact of Lewis's contribution to the problem of evil. As Dr.

Robert Walter Wall, associate professor of biblical studies at Seattle Pacific University, writes:

> Some Lewis scholars are quite willing to start and to stop with his more theological work, *The Problem of Pain*. Here one finds reasoned if not easy answers to all the problems inherent in the one. To stop here, however, is to miss the full measure of his teaching on the subject. In fact, while *Pain* is perhaps a masterpiece of Christian thoughtfulness, it simply does not do well alone. It desperately needs the emotive, subjective dimension to the problem Lewis provides in *A Grief Observed*. The point is this: If one is to understand suffering, he/she must understand that suffering cannot simply be dispatched to a world of reasoned stoicism. Yet when Lewis actually lives within the context of suffering and experiences pain first-hand, as *Grief* describes, he calls into question the legitimacy of and then finally extends those very beliefs developed in *Pain*. Two different contexts, two different treatments of the problem are brought into a profound dialectic that provides the reader with a more comprehensive picture of what is really at stake in human suffering.[2]

Our examination will thus cover two separate works that act as one. First, we will do a detailed survey of *The Problem of Pain* with special emphasis placed on Lewis's strongest and most relevant arguments. Second, we will cover the crucial themes in *A Grief Observed* as they relate to Lewis's personal response to pain and grief. And last, a brief critique and analysis of the major strongholds of Lewis's thinking will be examined, with a final word on application as we note the practical lessons of *A Grief Observed*.

Preface and Introduction

In his preface and introduction, Lewis sets the intellectual climate that shapes the following chapters about his thoughts on pain. From the start,

Lewis's work is an intellectual rather than experiential treatment of pain and suffering. He admits that he is stronger in acumen than in patience. Lewis writes:

> The only purpose of the book is to solve the intellectual problem raised by suffering; for the far higher task of teaching fortitude and patience I was never fool enough to suppose myself qualified, nor have I anything to offer my readers except my conviction that when pain is to be borne, a little courage helps more than much knowledge, a little human sympathy more than much courage, and the least tincture of the love of God more than all.[3]

From this admonition, Lewis moves to the origins of Christianity. He states:

> It must be understood that I am not primarily arguing the truth of Christianity but describing its origin—a task, in my view, necessary if we are to put the problem of pain in its right setting.[4]

Lewis then goes on to discuss the "three strands or elements"[5] that are common to all religions, with the exception that Christianity adds one unique strand. These strands consist of (1) the numinous (fear and awe), (2) morality (common concept of the "I ought" of right and wrong), and (3) the identification of the preceding two.[6] As for the fourth strand that is found exclusively in Christianity, Lewis describes the historical event. Concerning this event, Lewis writes:

> There was a man born among these Jews who claimed to be, or to be the son of, or to be "one with," the Something which is at once the awful haunter and the giver of the moral law. The claim is so shocking—a paradox, and even a horror, which we may easily be lulled into taking too lightly—that only two views of this man are possible. Either he was a raving lunatic of an unusually abominable

type, or He was, and is, precisely what He said. There is no middle way.[7]

Lewis seems to be saying that the historical event of the Incarnation, where God became a man in Christ, is the culmination and essence of the religious strands of awe and morality. The common strands became a common man as seen in the deity and humanity of Christ. What God did through the incarnation man could never do through "religion." Christianity is thus in a most unique position to solve the problem of evil because unlike religion, where man attempts to arrive at God through his own efforts, God once came to earth in Christ.

Subsequently, after his explanation of the historical incarnation, Lewis applies this incarnational fact by asserting one of the most profound and startling points of his book: that Christianity *creates* the problem of evil. Lewis writes:

> In a sense, it [Christianity] creates, rather than solves, the problem of pain, for pain would be no problem unless, side by side with our daily experience of this painful world, we had received what we think a good assurance that ultimate reality is righteous and loving.[8]

What Lewis is saying is significant. Without the Christian concept of a loving, all-wise, and all-powerful God, the problem of pain would not have arisen. The very word *problem* implies a contradiction between the pain of the world and the concept of a loving God. Christianity creates the problem of pain because it asserts the reality of evil and the reality of a good God in the same universe. There would be no problem if there was no Christian doctrine of both evil and a good God. Christianity creates the very problem that could in fact destroy its credibility.

However, for Lewis, the paradoxical nature of Christianity seems to give evidence for its very truth rather than its falsity. Commenting on this "ring of truth" that characterizes Christianity, Lewis states:

> And when we come to the last step of all, the historical Incarnation, the assurance is strongest of all. The story is

strangely like many myths which have haunted religion from the first, and yet it is not like them. It is not transparent to the reason; we could not have invented it ourselves…It has the master touch—the rough, male taste of reality, not made by us, or, indeed, for us, but hitting us in the face.[9]

It is with the preceding arguments that Lewis bases the remainder of his analysis of pain. He establishes the truth of Christianity before he discusses the "contradictions" of Christianity. Lewis shows that Christianity is not just one of many options in the religious market—rather, he shows that Christianity is the *only* option among "many." In short, he does his logical homework before he starts the lesson. Our task is now to turn to his nine lessons as seen in the remaining chapters of *The Problem of Pain*.

Divine Omnipotence

In this chapter, Lewis directs his thinking toward an analysis of God's power that includes a discussion of free will and possible worlds as they relate to omnipotence. He gives a brief yet precise definition of omnipotence:

His Omnipotence means power to do all that is intrinsically possible, not to do the intrinsically impossible. You may attribute miracles to Him, but not nonsense.[10]

And specifying his reference to "nonsense," Lewis states:

If you choose to say "God can give a creature free will and at the same time withhold free will from it," you have not succeeded in saying anything about God; meaningless combinations of words do not suddenly acquire meaning simply because we prefix to them the two other words "God can."[11]

Lewis, based on logic and semantics, is saying that God is capable of anything not contradictory if it does not fall into nonlogical categories. God does not create square circles, dry water, and married bachelors.

Lewis then correlates free will with omnipotence:

> We can, perhaps, conceive of a world in which God corrected the results of this abuse of free will by His creatures at every moment: so that a wooden beam became soft as grass when it was used as a weapon, and the air refused to obey me if I attempted to set up in it the sound waves that carry lies or insults. But such a world would be void; nay, if the principle were carried out to its logical conclusion.[12]

Lewis's argument is important and applicable. If God spent most of his time altering natural order to prevent evils, normal and functional life would be chaos. Granted, God's omnipotence can execute the needed miracles and interventions, but not at the expense of free will. God is able yet not willing because of man's will. Free will and the natural world are in a sense contingent upon one another. To jeopardize one at the expense of another would result in the total elimination of both free will and the natural order.

From free will, Lewis then moves to a discussion of possible worlds. In short, as the common question asks, is this the "best of all possible worlds?" Could God have created some other world that eliminates pain and suffering without the abuse of free will? Lewis proclaims:

> Perhaps this is not the "best of all possible" universes, but the only possible one. Possible worlds can mean only "worlds that God could have made, but didn't."[13]

One of Lewis's strongest points lies in the distinction between the "best" world and the "only" world. Mathematically, there are an infinite number of possible worlds, yet *morally*, there can only exist one actual world. According to Lewis, God's goodness, wisdom, and omnipotence eliminates the possibility of divine "confusion" concerning possible choices.

According to the perfection of God's nature and creation, this world is in a sense the best because it is the only actual world. God chose to create the actual world out of an infinite number of possible worlds.

Divine Goodness

At the outset of his chapter on God's goodness, Lewis discusses the semantic dilemma concerning "goodness."[14] According to Lewis, goodness may not mean exactly the same in the finite realm as it does in the divine realm. The confrontation with an absolute moral standard (God's goodness), causes one to note:

> The great test is that the recognition of the new standards [moral] is accompanied with the sense of shame and guilt: one is conscious of having blundered into society that one is unfit for. It is in the light of such experiences that we must consider the goodness of God. Beyond all doubt, His idea of "goodness" differs from ours.[15]

Lewis seems to be saying that our moral standards are seeds of God's standard, yet the fruition and actual modification of these seeds come when we base our morality on God's standard—not ours. It is as if God "appeals to our existing moral judgement."[16] When we thus become aware of this standard, its superiority is not hard to accept. It's a similar recipe, yet with superior ingredients.

From these introductory statements, Lewis begins a more detailed definition of divine goodness. By Lewis's standard, the common understanding of God's loving kindness is often insufficient. For Lewis, God's love is more than just kindness. In his classic style of lucidity and bluntness, Lewis writes:

> We want, in fact, not so much a Father in Heaven as a grandfather in heaven—a senile benevolence who, as they say, "liked to see young people enjoying themselves," and whose plan for the universe was simply that it might be truly said at the end of each day, "a good time was had by all."[17]

Lewis states further:

> If God is Love, He is by definition something more than
> mere kindness. And it appears, from all the records, that
> though He has often rebuked us and condemned us, He
> has never regarded us with contempt. He has paid us the
> intolerable compliment of loving us, in the deepest, most
> tragic, most inexorable sense.[18]

Often, as Lewis so insightfully notes, man places God in a preconceived "man upstairs" and "nice guy" stereotype. Man tries to approach God on man's terms rather than on God's terms. God is thus often reduced to a sentimental Santa Claus who is not concerned with upholding ethical absolutes. However, the God of biblical Christianity is indeed good and loving, yet this goodness and love is balanced with His judgment, justice, and holiness. God's love for man is "tragic," deep, intimate, and far more intricate than mere kindness. The divine love, as in all love, involved a risk and a cost that is indeed God's compliment and gift to mankind—the Lamb of God sacrificed for man.

To illustrate God's love for man, Lewis uses the popular example of a father's love for his son. He contrasts the authority/obedience distinctives of a father's love:

> Love between father and son, in this symbol, means
> essentially authoritative love on the one side, and obedient
> love on the other.[19]

Lewis later applies this father/son love to Christianity and the character of God's love for man. Lewis asserts:

> When Christianity says that God loves man, it means
> that God loves man: not that He has some "disinterested,"
> because really indifferent, concern for our welfare, but
> that, in awful and surprising truth, we are the objects of
> His love. You asked for a loving God: you have one.[20]

For Lewis, "the problem of reconciling human suffering with the existence of a God who loves is only insoluble so long as we attach a trivial meaning to the word *love*.[21] The fuel of Narnian love is ignited with a blend of the adjectives that Lewis utilizes in the preceding quotation. A loving God and a painful world can coexist if love is not seen as mere kindness. The real problem, according to Lewis, lies with definitions rather than Deity. For Lewis, it is a central thesis that "love may cause pain to its object, but only on the supposition that that object needs alteration to become fully lovable."[22]

It is this need for human alteration that Lewis's next chapter discusses.

Human Wickedness

From divine goodness, Lewis's next chapter shifts to human wickedness. He places wickedness in the context of the need for a "diagnosis" of the human condition. Because man no longer sees sin as the core of his problems, "Christianity now has to preach the diagnosis—in itself very bad news—before it can win a hearing for the cure."[23] The central thesis of this chapter Lewis states in retrospect as follows:

> I have been aiming at an intellectual, not an emotional, effect: I have been trying to make the reader believe that we actually are, at present, creatures whose character must be, in some respects, a horror to God, as it is, when we really see it, a horror to ourselves.[24]

Modern man must thus see his disease before a cure is possible.

To explain this modern distortion toward sin, Lewis cites two reasons to aid in both analysis and application. First, modern man equates kindness with happiness. Because some humans can attribute kindness to themselves for never doing anything "bad," and they equate this "kindness" with goodness, Lewis writes:

> Thus a man easily comes to console himself for all his other vices by a conviction that "his heart's in the right place" and "he wouldn't hurt a fly," though in fact he has

> never made the slightest sacrifice for a fellow creature. We
> think we are kind when we are only happy.[25]

Secondly, the influx of psychoanalytic presuppositions on the public mind dilutes the impact of the word *sin*. The real danger in such thinking is that what "they [psycho-analytic proponents] have actually left on most people is that the sense of Shame is a dangerous and mischievous thing."[26] Humans are thus encouraged to openly expose their "inner conflicts" as a means of relieving a false sense of guilt. Yet, according to Lewis, "unless Christianity is wholly false, the perception of ourselves which we have in moments of shame must be the only true one."[27]

Furthermore, Lewis stresses that "a recovery of the old sense of sin is essential to Christianity."[28] Lewis states:

> Christ takes for granted that men are bad. Until we really
> feel this assumption of His to be true, though we are
> part of the world He came to save, we are not part of the
> audience to whom His words are addressed.[29]

Thus, for Lewis, an accurate appraisal of sin is essential for both the diagnosis and cure of man's wickedness. For pain to be placed in its proper perspective, human sin must never be reduced to mere "altered" or "suppressed" feelings. Sin is sin. There is little room for optimism concerning a cure of human nature without accepting Christ's view of wickedness.

To close this chapter on human wickedness, Lewis seals his case against the modern view of sin by stating eight reasons in support of human sinfulness. First, modern man looks to the outside rather than the inside for sin. Every person has a silent and inward wickedness that is hidden to the public eye.[30] Second, man lightens sin by excusing it through corporate or social guilt.[31] Third, some think that duration or time will erase sin.[32] Fourth, man attempts to justify sin through a "safety in numbers" mentality.[33] Fifth, different ages in history have excelled in virtue, yet to God, all ages are caught in wickedness and in need of redemption.[34] Sixth, modern man attempts to equate virtue with kindness, but true kindness involves all virtues. Seventh, Christianity is not just a "moral teaching," rather, it demands personal holiness in reference to God's holiness.[35] And lastly, God must never be blamed for any style of evolutionary mentality that says "badness is an unavoidable legacy from our animal ancestors."[36]

The Fall of Man

After determining the wickedness of man, Lewis turns to the origin of human wickedness: the Fall of man. Lewis defines the Fall as follows:

> According to that doctrine, man is now a horror to God and to himself and a creature ill-adapted to the universe not because God made him so but because he has made himself so by the abuse of his free will.[37]

The thesis of this chapter is that man, as a species, spoiled himself, and that good, to us in our present state, must therefore mean primarily remedial or corrective good.[38]

To preserve this good, man often asks, "Why did God not intervene to prevent the Fall of man?" To this, Lewis answers:

> It would, no doubt, have been possible for God to remove by miracle the results of the first sin committed by a human being; but this would not have been much good unless He was prepared to remove the results of the second sin, and of the third, and so on forever.[39]

Lewis's point is crucial to an effective treatment of pain and suffering. The options are clear: either man is free, or he is determined. A world governed by miracle at the moment of every choice would be a playground of human puppets. It would mean a miracle will rather than a free will. God would thus have to alter both the natural order and man's will to attain a sinless world.

From this preceding point, Lewis discusses modern science and its archaeological *post hoc proper hoc* fallacies.[40] He also touches on pride as the greatest sin of man.[41] A lengthy, speculative description of the Fall in "unbaptized" terminology is also included.[42] Lewis further describes the

Fall by answering the question: "How could a paradisal man fall?" He declares:

> This act of self-will on the part of the creature, which constitutes an utter falseness to its true creaturely position, is the only sin that can be conceived as the fall.[43]

According to Lewis, the "self" is the fuel which fired the Fall. A choice for or against God constituted the option of a fall, even amid the innocence of the garden. From the start, man had the choice of bowing before God or man. The apparent "flaw" of creation thus produced a worthwhile yet risky world. Part of this risk resulted in the next subject of Lewis's work: human pain.

Human Pain

Lewis's two chapters on human pain supply the nucleus of his entire analysis of pain. From the onset, Lewis is clear that man rather than God is responsible for much of human suffering. Men, not God, make the tools and toys of suffering. He writes:

> It is men, not God, who have produced racks, whips, prisons, slavery, guns, bayonets, and bombs; it is by human avarice or human stupidity, not by the churlishness of nature, that we have poverty and overwork.[44]

After placing some, but not all the blame for pain on man,[45] Lewis articulates a twofold definition of pain:

> The truth is that the word Pain has two senses which must now be distinguished. a. A particular kind of sensation, probably conveyed by specialized nerve fibers and recognizable by the patient as that kind of sensation whether he dislikes it or not. b. Any experience, whether physical or mental, which the patient dislikes.[46]

Lewis's definition of pain is thus divided into two categories. First, the physical symptoms of pain. And second, the discomfort of pain, be it physical or mental. Both categories interrelate, especially when physical pain is raised to a higher level of severity.

In addition to Lewis's clinical definition of pain, he also gives a sermonic or didactic definition of suffering:

> Pain insists upon being attended to. God whispers to us
> in our pleasures, speaks in our conscience, but shouts in
> our pains: it is His megaphone to rouse a deaf world.[47]

Here Lewis describes the truthful yet harsh reality of pain as a stimulant to wake apathy. Pain, for Lewis, unveils the rebel will and leaves it bare before reality. Pain can be a divine tool that awakens the hardest of hearts. Pain is the divine sound amid human silence.

After his discussion of the didactic aspects of suffering, Lewis touches on the practical ramifications of pain. He proposes three operations of suffering. First, retribution can instill good results. For men to make punishment appropriate for only the "guilty" or criminals is illogical because "by so doing they render all punishment unjust."[48] Second, God brings suffering to draw us from happiness and prosperity to Himself. Unfortunately, "we find God an interruption" amid the common pleasures of life.[49] And third, suffering teaches one obedience to the will of God despite our preferences.[50] As a personal illustration to at least two of the preceding three points, Lewis, with compelling candor, writes:

> Thus the terrible necessity of tribulation is only too clear.
> God has had me for but forty-eight hours and then only
> by dint of taking everything else away from me. Let Him
> but sheath that sword for a moment and I behave like a
> puppy when the hated bath is over—I shake myself as dry
> as I can and race off to reacquire my comfortable dirtiness,
> if not in the nearest manure heap, at least in the nearest
> flowerbed.[51]

For Lewis, although pain is a profoundly serious matter and is not to be taken lightly, suffering can and does produce good. It seems that pain is most effective in uprooting the prideful self of its egocentric throne. Lewis admits that "I have seen great beauty of spirit in some who were great sufferers. I have seen men, for the most part, grow better not worse with advancing years, and I have seen the last illness produce treasures of fortitude and meekness from most unpromising subjects."[52]

According to Lewis, suffering seems to immediately clean away the obstacles that blind one to what is important in life. Pain, and pain alone, has its special way of setting priorities straight. Suffering can indeed produce good.

Human Pain, continued

In chapter 7, Lewis advances six propositions concerning suffering. First, suffering can have a redemptive effect:

> But if suffering is good, ought it not to be pursued rather than avoided? I answer that suffering is not good in itself. What is good in any painful experience is, for the sufferer, his submission to the will of God, and, for the spectators, the compassion aroused and the acts of mercy to which it leads.[53]

To illustrate this submission and compassion, Lewis uses a Judas/John comparison. Lewis believes that the crucifixion itself is the best, as well as the worst, of all historical events, but the role of Judas remains simply evil. For you will certainly carry out God's purpose, however you act, but it makes a difference to you whether you serve like Judas or like John.[54]

One's choice is thus to respond to suffering by rebellion or submission. A servant attitude toward suffering by no means answers all questions regarding suffering, but it does set a practical basis from which pain may be bearable. In short, "the redemptive effect of suffering lies chiefly in its tendency to reduce the rebel will."[55]

Second, Lewis proposes that an eternal "reform" of the world will not end suffering. He asserts:

If tribulation is a necessary element in redemption, we must anticipate that it will never cease till God sees that world to be either redeemed or no further redeemable. A Christian cannot, therefore, believe any of those who promise that if only some reform in our economic, political, or hygienic system were made, a heaven on earth would follow.[56]

The Christian must thus guard himself from thinking that "external" progress will eventually produce redemption. The self, a concept that Lewis consistently speaks of, can only be transformed from the inside—not the outside—of man. "Heaven on earth" will never occur until heaven takes residence in the heart of man. "Heaven on earth" was and will be Christ on earth.

Third, politics and the Christian concept of self-surrender must not be mixed. For Lewis, "the Christian doctrine of self-surrender and obedience are purely theological, and not in the least a political doctrine."[57]

Fourth, only God can satisfy the deepest longings of the human heart. Lewis believes that the security we crave would teach us to rest our hearts in this world and pose an obstacle to our return to God; a few moments of happy love, a landscape, a symphony, a merry meeting with our friends, a bath, or a football match have no such tendency. Our Father refreshes us on the journey with some pleasant inns but will not encourage us to mistake them for home.[58]

Fifth, the degree of pain is different from the quality of pain. Suffering should not reflect addition. Lewis states:

> There is no such thing as a sum of suffering, for no one suffers it. When we have reached the maximum that a single person can suffer, we have, no doubt, reached something very horrible, but we have reached all the suffering there ever can be in the universe.[59]

And lastly, "of all evils, pain only is sterilized or disinfected evil."[60] Unlike sin or error, pain does not spread to bystanders. For Lewis, it is important that suffering naturally produces in the spectators (unless they are unusually depraved) no bad effect, but a good one—pity. Thus, that evil which God chiefly uses to produce the "complex good" is most markedly disinfected, or deprived of that proliferous tendency that is the worst characteristic of evil in general.[61]

Hence, from redemption to addition, the preceding remarks reveal that Lewis saw pain as able to produce both good and neutral effects. Yet, there remains one consequence of evil that is vital to Lewis's canon on pain: the doctrine of hell. It is to this doctrine we now turn.

Hell

Lewis's entire concept of hell seems to closely follow a pointed aphorism of George McDonald, which states: "The one principle of hell is—'I am my own.'"[62] Lewis argues that the reality of hell is supported by scripture, Christ, and logic. Yet, if he were able, "there is no doctrine which [he] would more willingly remove from Christianity than this."[63] For Lewis, the doctrine of hell is not tolerable—it is *moral*.

One of the central factors that shapes Lewis's doctrine on hell is free will. He bluntly writes:

> If a game is played, it must be possible to lose it. I would pay any price to be able to say truthfully "All will be saved." But my reason retorts, "Without their will, or with it?"[64]

With logic and lucidity, Lewis makes a crucial point. The choice is either determinism or free will.[65] The logical implications of universalism (that all will eventually be saved) would thus eliminate free will. Determinism and universalism are unacceptable; free will is moral and logically consistent.

From free will, Lewis asserts that hell is morally justifiable. He believes so for five reasons. First, retributive punishment is not always wrong. For example, an evil man who never feels guilt or remorse, despite his evil deeds, often thinks "that God and man are fools whom he has got the better of."[66] Should such a man be forever placed in heavenly bliss? No, says Lewis. When the "conflict between Justice and Mercy"[67] arises, justice is a moral necessity. Lewis then makes one of the most important moral distinctions of this chapter: the distinction between condoning and forgiving. He writes:

> The demand that God should forgive such a man while he remains what he is, is based on a confusion between condoning and forgiving. To condone an evil is simply to ignore it, to treat it as if it were good.[68]

Hence, hell is a just and logical destiny for one who ignores both guilt and forgiveness.

Second, Lewis touches on the common speculation that death is not final, thus one should receive a "second chance." This objection is answered by arguing that finality eventually becomes ultimate. Lewis argues:

> I believe that if a million chances were likely to do good, they would be given. But a master often knows, when boys and parents do not, that it is really useless to send a boy in for a certain examination again.[69]

Third, Lewis speaks of the severity of hell. Damnation, utter darkness, and the image of fire must not be taken lightly. Even if there are to be both eternal agony and pleasure in hell, "that black pleasure would be such as to send any soul, not already damned, flying to its prayers in nightmare terror: even if there were pains in heaven, all who understand would desire them."[70]

Fourth, it is often objected that "no charitable man could himself be blessed in heaven while he knew that even one human soul was still in hell; and if so, are we more merciful than God?"[71] Yet, Lewis argues that the issue here is not time, but instead finality. The condemned soul must face the eternal consequences of its choices.

Fifth, some object that one lost soul equals the failure of omnipotence. "And so it does," Lewis writes. However, he immediately interjects free will in answer to this objection:

> I willingly believe that the damned are, in one sense, successful, rebels to in the end; that the doors of hell are locked on the inside.[72]

In his picturesque yet bold way, Lewis sees the damned as locking the door of hell with their own volitional key. Omnipotence will not violate the privacy of free will, and thus God cannot be held responsible for "sending people to hell."

Lewis closes his chapter by posing a pointed question to any skeptic concerning the reality of hell. He writes:

> In the long run the answer to all those who object to the doctrine of hell is itself a question: "What are you asking God to do?" To wipe out their past sins and, at all costs, to give them a fresh start, smoothing every difficulty and offering every miraculous help? But He has done so, on Calvary. To forgive them? They will not be forgiven. To leave them alone? Alas, I am afraid that is what He does.[73]

Animal Pain

In his ninth chapter, Lewis touches on an interesting yet speculative aspect of suffering: animal pain. At first, one might ask, "Just how does animal pain have any bearing on evil and suffering?" If animals have instinct rather than a soul endowed with free will, why do they suffer? Although we have no biblical data on pain's relationship to the animal kingdom, Lewis notes three important points. First, what does an animal feel when it is experiencing pain? To answer this, Lewis makes a distinction between *sentience* and *consciousness*. Sentience represents feeling or sensation, whereas consciousness would amount to perception or thought. Animals experience sentience, but not consciousness. Humans experience sentience, but they can also cognitively interpret such sensations with the conscious mind. Lewis writes:

> How far up the scale such unconscious sentience may extend, I will not even guess. It is certainly difficult to suppose that the apes, the elephant, and higher domestic animals, have not, in some degree, a self or soul which connects experiences and gives rise to rudimentary individuality.[74]

Second, Lewis believes the origin of animal suffering may be related to the Fall. He also speculates that Satan may have corrupted the animal creation before man arrived on the scene.[75]

Third, Lewis discusses the immortality of animals. Again, he speculates that sanctified men may pass on immortality to their pets through being their masters. Lewis realizes that "the real difficulty about supposing most animals to be immortal is that immortality has almost no meaning for a creature which is not 'conscious.'"[76] An animal may feel APNI, but it cannot spell PAIN.

Heaven

In the final chapter of his work, Lewis closes with a brief analysis of heaven. He aptly states the application of heaven to the problem of suffering and pain:

> A book on suffering which says nothing of heaven, is leaving out almost the whole of one side of the account. Scripture and tradition habitually put the joys of heaven into the scale against the sufferings of earth, and no solution of the problem of pain which does not do so can be called a Christian one.[77]

For Lewis, heaven balances the scale of pain with the "weight of glory." He does not base this doctrine on optimistic sentiment. Heaven is a certain reality because it is contingent upon the truth of Christianity. Because Christianity is true, heaven is real.

Lewis also places great stress on the truth that man is made for heaven like "a glove is made for a hand."[78] The self will never find its rest until that which it deeply longs for is fulfilled. Furthermore, the thought that man does not really desire heaven is just an illusion. Heaven is made for man and man for heaven. The "rebel will," through obedience, humility, and submission to Christ, does have a home for its deepest desires.

H. STUART ATKINS

A Grief Observed: An Experiential Approach to Pain

Although Lewis's work *The Problem of Pain* is of monumental importance for understanding pain, his canon is not complete without a brief analysis of his book *A Grief Observed*. In *A Grief Observed*, the intellectual fortress of Lewis's thought is shattered through the tragic suffering and loss of his wife. In fact, the grief he faced nearly brought intellectual and personal abandonment of his Christianity. He thus composed a short diary to preserve his sanity during such a trying time. This diary was later published as *A Grief Observed*.

Dr. Wall summarizes well the impact of *A Grief Observed*:

> *Grief* is Lewis' second and less pretentious book on suffering. It is also the more important. In it the orderly world made of theology and reason that he constructed in *Pain* is threatened by the loss of his wife Joy. It is a grinding grief of the kind that immobilizes one in an apparent hopeless and isolated reality. There really is no future in such grieving. There is no thought given to benefits or to God's purpose for it all. Everything is in disarray, and all is consumed by a self-centered pathos. Life is really not life at all, because life itself was so wrapped up in what is lost. One cannot act too wisely, if at all, during crises of grief. He is in bondage to his grief with little hope for escape. The bridge to recovery has to be built by someone or something else.[79]

This short work is divided into four sections, which act as progressive phases of Lewis's experience. First, Lewis feels the frustrations of the fear, doubt, loneliness, and apathy that accompany grief.[80] The memories of the past destroy the security of common sense. In addition, Lewis experiences a laziness that is difficult to overcome.

From these initial experiences, Lewis expresses the deep, personal, subjective, and melancholic emotions he faced during his grief. Amid his confusion, the question of God arrives on the scene as he writes:

Meanwhile, where, is God? This is one of the most disquieting symptoms. When you are happy, so happy that you have no sense of needing Him, so happy that you are tempted to feel His claims upon you as an interruption, if you remember yourself and turn to Him with gratitude and praise, you will be—or so it feels—welcomed with open arms. But go to Him when your need is desperate, when all other help is vain, and what do you find? A door slammed in your face, and a sound of bolting and double bolting on the inside. After that, silence. You may as well turn away. The longer you wait, the more emphatic the silence will become. There are no lights in the windows. It might be an empty house. Was it ever inhabited? It seemed so once. And that seeming was as strong as this. What can this mean? Why is He so present a commander in our time of prosperity and so very absent a help in time of trouble?[81]

In the preceding thoughts, God's megaphone of pain brings nothing but meaningless silence for Lewis. Prosperity brings divine presence—or so it seems—and grief brings divine silence. Lewis feels utterly alone and locked into doubt and frustration. It was not that he doubted God's existence; rather, it was "coming to believe such dreadful things about Him"[82] that worried Lewis. He was thus more concerned about divine sadism than personal atheism. Lewis seems to feel that God is an evil genius who has played a cosmic joke on him.[83] Because of his initial grief, he is caught in doubt and despair.

In phase two, evaluation and cynicism arise; Lewis realizes how tragedy is a potent test of faith. Insightfully, he writes:

You never know how much you really believe anything until its truth or falsehood becomes a matter of life and death to you. It is easy to say you believe a rope to be strong and sound as long as you are merely using it to cord a box. But suppose you had to hang by that rope over a precipice. Wouldn't you then first discover how much you really trusted it? Only a real risk tests the reality of a belief.[84]

Lewis also found little comfort in the common aphorisms by which friends would attempt to console him. At one point, he was even tempted to demand of God: "God forgive God."[85] In addition, the goodness of God was also found suspect during Lewis's grief. He writes:

> Sooner or later I must face the question in plain language. What reason have we, except our own desperate wishes, to believe that God is, by any standard we can conceive, "good"? Doesn't all the *prima facie* evidence suggest exactly the opposite? What have we to set against it? I wrote last night. It was a yell rather than a thought, let me try it over again. Is it rational to believe in a bad God? Anyway, in a God so bad as all that? The Cosmic Sadist, the spiteful imbecile?[86]

Lewis was thus battling between his Christianity and cynicism. His blunt and, at times, abominable attitudes brought him to depths of honesty and personal irony. Because of grief, God's goodness, which was supported in *The Problem of Pain*, now became suspect and questionable. The foundations of Lewis's thinking were assaulted by the severity of his emotions, doubts, and personal experience.

The third and fourth phase of grief brings Lewis to a point of reconciliation and understanding. His anger toward God seems to subside and he begins to fathom why his thoughts and emotions took such a negative and potentially destructive course. Concerning God as a "cosmic sadist," Lewis writes:

> All that stuff about the Cosmic Sadist was not so much the expression of thought as of hatred. I was getting from it the only pleasure a man in anguish can get; the pleasure of hitting back. It was really just Billingsgate—mere abuse; "telling God what I thought of Him." And of course, as in all abusive language, "what I thought" didn't mean what I thought true.[87]

Lewis then compares grief to physical pain. Grief to him is far worse than physical pain. He asserts:

> What is grief compared with physical pain? Whatever fools may say, the body can suffer twenty times more than the mind. The mind has always some power of evasion. At worst, the unbearable thought only comes back and back, but the physical pain can be absolutely continuous. Thought is never static; pain often is.[88]

Lewis's thoughts were the greatest threat to his faith. Despite the truth to which his mind was committed, his thoughts would still betray him in times of grief and sorrow. Ironically, truth became captive to negative thoughts. The very passage through which truth flows—the thought—became "nontruth." His mind thus seemed to resort to "verbal revenge" toward God. Revenge became the servant of thought rather than thought the servant of truth.

Lewis eventually concludes that the goodness of God necessitates human suffering. God in His goodness brings trials to show *us* the quality of our faith. Concerning these trials, Lewis asserts that the tortures occur. If they are unnecessary, then there is no God or a bad one. If there is a good God, then these tortures are necessary. For no even moderately good Being could possibly inflict or permit them if they weren't.[89]

Lewis further writes:

> God has not been trying an experiment on my faith or love in order to find out their quality. He knew it already. It was I who didn't. In this trial He makes us occupy the dock, the witness box, and the bench all at once. He always knew that my temple was a house of cards. His only way of making me realize the fact was to knock it down.[90]

Lewis seems to be saying that he, not God was the problem. God was more interested in Lewis's *response* to grief than the grief itself. What at first seemed to erode his faith actually strengthened it. Grief became a building block rather than a stumbling stone. Only the hindsight of traveling through such grief could reveal its didactic purpose.

The best way to explain what Lewis learned through his grief may be summarized in his classic statement: "He [God] is the great iconoclast." Indeed, it was God who attacked Lewis's established "beliefs" and divine "images." He writes:

> My idea of God is not a divine idea. It has to be shattered time after time. He shatters it Himself. He is the great iconoclast. Could we not almost say that this shattering is one of the marks of His presence? The Incarnation is the supreme example; it leaves all previous ideas of the Messiah in ruins. And most are "offended" by the iconoclasm; and blessed are those who are not.[91]

In the end, Lewis bows before his omnipotent, good, and omniscient creator with an admirable mental humility. Lewis knew his epistemological limitations. And yet, often only grief will teach the griever such lessons. With his faith near restoration and his confidence in God intact, Lewis writes:

> When I lay these questions before God I get no answer. But a rather special sort of "No answer." It is not the locked door. It is more like a silent, certainly not uncompassionate, gaze. As though He shook His head not in refusal but waiving the question. ...
>
> Can a mortal ask questions which God finds unanswerable? Quite easily, I should think. All nonsense questions are unanswerable. How many hours are there in a mile? Is yellow square or round? Probably half the questions we ask—half our great theological and metaphysical problems—are like that.
>
> And now that I come to think of it, there's no practical problem before me at all. I know the two great commandments, and I'd better get on with them.[92]

Critique, Analysis, and Conclusion

In the preceding analysis of Lewis's apologetic toward pain and suffering, one notes that both *The Problem of Pain* and *A Grief Observed* offer a powerful justification of biblical theism. After presenting Lewis's basic position, additional comments serve to further clarify, support, and constructively criticize his position on pain.

Because the important issues Lewis raises are numerous, a brief appraisal of his strongest and most dominant arguments is needed. Overall, Lewis's treatment of pain and suffering is no doubt one of the most concise, intelligent, and penetrating presentations written during the twentieth century. Concerning the quality and impact of Lewis on modern man and his thinking, Dr. Robert Houston Smith writes:

> Lewis must be credited with making one of the most sophisticated, consistent, and elegant explanations of supernaturalism in the twentieth century. He devised his Christian objectivism brilliantly and presented it in the most diverse and delightful array of garments imaginable. That philosophy of religion appears not only in his apologetic writings but in virtually all of his other words as well, including his respected studies of English literature, over a span of more than thirty years. His intellect was one of the keenest of his day; his capacity for reading, absorbing, and critically evaluating what he read was enormous, and in addition he was gifted with an extraordinary ability to think logically and rapidly and to write skillfully. All of these qualities he put to the fullest use.[93]

Furthermore, such brilliance and quality that Johnson speaks of is clearly seen in *The Problem of Pain*, especially in the first eight chapters of this work. The late Talmage C. Johnson, in his 1950 review of Lewis's work on pain, writes:

> In the main, one does not find such grounds [logical]
> for challenging the first eight chapters of this book. The
> argument for faith in the goodness and wisdom of the
> Creator is consistent and well put. The contention that
> Omnipotence cannot do the intrinsically impossible is
> sound. The nature of divine goodness and of human
> freedom is adequately treated, nor can there be much
> disagreement with the notion that pain is rooted both in
> the fixed order of nature, essential for a society of souls,
> and in the abuse of freedom by man the creature. The
> use of pain for creative and redemptive purposes is made
> clear.[94]

Although the preceding comments concerning Lewis give both a positive and general evaluation of his work, there is further need for a more specific analysis. First, some brief remarks on the central arguments and doctrines Lewis utilizes will shape our critique. Second, we will describe the overall strengths of Lewis's approach.

Free Will

One of Lewis's most convincing arguments is his free will defense. Throughout *The Problem of Pain*, free will is consistently correlated with many of the major criticisms against Christianity. In Lewis's canon on pain, free will is the cornerstone of his approach. Free will is a thread that unites the whole of Lewis's writing. Commenting on the strength of Lewis's use of free will, the late head of the department of philosophy at the University of London, Dr. Joad, writes:

> Granting pain to be evil, perhaps the greatest of evils, I
> have come to accept the Christian view of pain as not
> incompatible with the Christian concept of the Creator
> and of the world that He has made. That view I take
> to be briefly as follows: It was of no interest to God to
> create a species consisting of virtuous automata, for the
> "virtue" of automata who can do no other that they do

is a courtesy title only; it is analogous to the "virtue" of the stone that rolls downhill or of the water that freezes at 32 degrees. To what end, it may be asked, should God create such creatures? That He might be praised by them? But automatic praise is a mere succession of noises. That He might love them? But they are essentially unlovable; you cannot love puppets. And so God gave man free will that he might increase in virtue by his own efforts and become, as a free moral being, a worthy object of God's love. Freedom entails freedom to go wrong: man did, in fact, go wrong, misusing God's gift and doing evil. Pain is a by-product of evil; and so pain came into the world as a result of man's misuse of God's gift of free will.

So much I can understand; so much, indeed, I accept. It is plausible; it is rational; it hangs together.[95]

Although Joad was in strong disagreement regarding Lewis's view of animal pain, they were friends despite their polemical battles. Joad, in support of Lewis, argues there is no middle ground between free will or determinism.[96] One must accept one or the other. Because determinism is not logical, free will is both plausible and logical. Lewis's position on free will, thus, stands as one of the most potent of his writing.

Sin: The Recovery of Our Sense of It

With boldness Lewis argues against the grain of modern thinking in one essential doctrine: sin.[97] For Lewis, sin was not just an ancient myth—it is a present reality that resulted from the Fall. Sin is not a bystander in human pain; rather, pain is a direct descendant of man's will and heart. Consequently, while at Cambridge, Lewis was responsible for reminding all that "nobody at Cambridge seems to have heard of original sin until quite lately."[98]

Although Lewis is bold in his treatment of sin, he seems to lack theological precision in his explanation of total depravity. He thinks the phrase "total depravity" is flawed because the word *total* implies that, in such a state, man could not recognize his depravity. In short, Lewis thinks such a phrase eliminates human goodness. However, it seems that Lewis misunderstands the full application of this doctrine. Commenting on Lewis's interpretation of human depravity, Richard B. Cunningham notes:

> The doctrine, in fact, does not deny that there is some goodness in human nature; it basically argues that man's will is in bondage, and every virtue is tainted by pride. Ironically, in other places Lewis does reject the heart of the doctrine (without apparently knowing it), when he denies that man's will is in bondage and that he is unable to turn to God. Paradisal Man, in Lewis' view, could still turn back to God, though only by painful effort because his natural inclination was selfward. Here is an example of Lewis' occasional insufficient grasp of the finer points of theology.[99]

Lewis, thus, occasionally suffered from his lack of background in formal theology. His training in both philosophy and literature were valuable tools for his interpretation of the ideas and linguistics of scripture, yet at times his theological understanding lacked in detail.

Hell and Heaven

Usually the terms hell and heaven are placed in reverse order. However, for Lewis, placing the chapter on hell before the chapter on heaven seems to be no mistake in *The Problem of Pain*. Hell, for Lewis, was the volitional and moral rebellion of the self, which resulted in the most serious of consequences. Since the reality of hell in the context of a good and loving God seemed contradictory, Lewis saw the utter importance of a chapter on this topic.

His point that hell is a moral rather than an "unloving" alternative of free will is crucial. Man is not "sent" to hell; he chooses hell. The "rebel will" that Lewis so often speaks of is the vehicle to hell—not God. Furthermore, what makes Lewis's point so strong is that he appeals to moral necessity rather than just "fire and brimstone." Men may or may not fear fire and brimstone, yet all men must function in a moral world.

However, Lewis brings hope concerning hell—namely, heaven. The reality of pain may force one to patience to endure, yet there is a certain hope for the "rebel wills" of those who choose to submit rather than cling to the self. There is an antithesis to hell, yet it takes the form of a moral choice instead of some dualistic option or opposite. Lewis leaves the reader with a balance regarding the moral and eternal consequences of choice: either heaven or hell as embodied in one's freedom to choose either.

Animal Pain

When Lewis turns to the beast and pain, he also turns to speculation. Because this topic finds no mention in scripture, Lewis is quick to admit his speculation. Yet, even amid the speculative categories, Lewis makes a bold attempt to answer some perplexing issues. In addition, Lewis's personal care for and mixed concern for the animal world was apparent. The late Kathern Lindskoog writes:

> Sometimes Lewis experienced such pity and indignation over the incessant suffering of animals that every argument for the existence of a good God sounded hollow. The insect world in particular (Lewis loathed large spiders) sometimes seems to be hell itself, teeming with pain.[100]

Probably the most cogent critique of Lewis's position on animals is that of C. E. M. Joad, who was referred to earlier.

First, Joad asserts that pain is pain, no matter who or what is experiencing it. "Pain is felt even if there is no continuing ego to feel it and to relate it to past and to future pains."[101]

Second, Joad has problems with Lewis's definition of sentience as a continuation of sense experience. Animals do indeed remember past pains; thus we must not take such pains to be mere "sensations." A presupposition that "no continuing consciousness presupposes no memory"[102] is a major fault of Lewis's thinking.

And third, Joad applies the reverse application of Lewis's concept that immortal selfhood may be passed from master to animal. It seems obvious that "if one animal may attain good immortal selfhood in and through a good man, he may attain bad immortal selfhood in and through a bad man."[103] Hence, immortality in believing men does not imply its transfer to the animal kingdom.

It thus seems that Lewis's speculation concerning animal pain led to some awkward conclusions. It may have been safer to adhere to that which scripture directly or indirectly supports, which in the case of animals is almost nothing. Fortunately, Lewis admits his speculation at the onset, thus he by no means was dogmatic on such an assumptive issue.

Overall, Lewis's *The Problem of Pain* exemplifies one of the most effective and brief treatments of this crucial issue. Lewis's work, although not without its faults, must command the upmost respect and admiration. With logic, humility, acumen, honesty, balance, and doctrinal validity, Lewis has produced a mind-changing book. There are few men in history who have so insightfully and effectively dealt with pain and suffering in just 154 pages. The skeptic must not only be encouraged to read this work; he or she must be warned that the completion of the last page may be the end of his or her skepticism.

Lessons from A Grief Observed

Our final critique of Lewis ends with his *experiential* response to pain in *A Grief Observed*. From this second and retrospective work on suffering, we can make a series of applications, as Lewis himself made following the death of his wife. From the lessons that follow, one notes the essential balance that *A Grief Observed* brings to Lewis's writings on pain.

First, there are no easy answers to grief and pain. It is unwise to utter "spiritual" and pointed aphorisms to comfort the grieved. There are times when "dropping" Bible verses on a grieved ear will cause confusion and more questions rather than comfort.

Second, when pain or innocent suffering brings grief, expect emotion turmoil in varying degrees. Often, grief is normal rather than abnormal. However, try not to let your grief overwhelm you.

Third, do not be alarmed from your varied emotional responses to pain or suffering. Do not always trust your immediate mental or emotional response to grief. Try to let truth guard emotions rather than emotions decay truth.

Fourth, do not fear complete and bold honesty with God. Tell Him how you feel and think. Silence with God is merely delaying what He already knows you are thinking.

Fifth, remember the difference between doubt and denial. Doubt is a testing of the truth; denial is a rebellion from the truth.

Sixth, remember that God is indeed the great Iconoclast. God is often more appalled at surface "religious" solutions to suffering than we are ourselves.

Seventh, suffering and pain may often be a refinement and purification of our faith. Allow time, patience, hindsight, and prayer to supply their gradual answers.

Eighth, there is both an emotional and an intellectual response to grief. Try to let truth come before experience rather than experience before truth. The subjective does play a part, yet the balance of Lewis's intellect and emotions is a lesson for us all.

And last, we must not try to "tame" our concept of God. The Father of our Lord Jesus Christ must not be placed into a neat, categorical box that dictates all the hows and whys of His divine will and purposes. We must never forget that,

> the real problem of observed pain is that in our bereavement we want God domesticated. We want to make sense of our difficult reality by making our kind of simplified sense of Him. What is needed is not a partner in grief but one who stands outside of it all, so that in His freedom from all that immobilizes He is able to free us. Often it is in appealing to a notion of God, as Lewis tried unsuccessfully to do, that we fail to hear the "real" Him speak words of comfort to us. Thus, it is not the perceived silence of God that is ultimately the problem, but it is the noise of our own wailing and railing at him that needs to be silenced, because in pain the silence of man would

better do. It is not so much knowing how the goodness of God interfaces with the reality of suffering that counts. Rather, it is simply knowing that the goodness of God is somehow present in all this mess, and that He is with us in power.[104]

NOTES

1   C. S. Lewis, *A Grief Observed* (Toronto: Bantam Books, 1961), 28.
2   Robert Walter Wall, "The Problem of Observed Pain: A Study of C.S. Lewis on Suffering," *Journal of the Evangelical Theological Society* 26, no. 4 (December 1983): 444.
3   C. S. Lewis, *The Problem of Pain* (New York: Macmillan, 1962), 10.
4   *Ibid.*, 16
5   *Ibid.*
6   *Ibid.*, 16-23.
7   *Ibid.*, 23-24.
8   *Ibid.*, 24.
9   *Ibid.*, 25.
10 *Ibid.*, 28.
11 *Ibid.*
12 *Ibid.*, 33-34.
13 *Ibid.*, 35.
14 *Ibid.*, 37-38.
15 *Ibid.*, 38-39.
16 *Ibid.*, 39.
17 *Ibid.*, 40.
18 *Ibid.*, 40-41.
19 *Ibid.*, 45.
20 *Ibid.*, 46-47.
21 *Ibid.*, 47.
22 *Ibid.*, 55.
23 *Ibid.*
24 *Ibid.*, 67.
25 *Ibid.*, 56.
26 *Ibid.*
27 *Ibid.*, 57.
28 *Ibid.*
29 *Ibid.*
30 *Ibid.*, 59-60.
31 *Ibid.*, 60-61.
32 *Ibid.*, 61-62.
33 *Ibid.*, 62-64.
34 *Ibid.*, 64.
35 *Ibid.*, 65.

36 *Ibid.*, 66.

37 *Ibid.*, 69.

38 *Ibid.*, 88.

39 *Ibid.*, 71.

40 *Ibid.*, 72-74.

41 *Ibid.*, 75.

42 *Ibid.*, 77-86.

43 *Ibid.*, 80-81.

44 *Ibid.*, 89.

45 Lewis is fully aware that not all pain can be traced to human sinfulness: "But there remains, nonetheless, much suffering which cannot thus be traced to ourselves. Even if all suffering were man-made, we should like to know the reason for the enormous permission to torture their fellows which God gives to the worst of men."[Lewis, *Problem of Pain*, 89.]

46 *Ibid.*, 90.

47 *Ibid.*, 93-95.

48 *Ibid.*, 94.

49 *Ibid.*, 96.

50 *Ibid.*, 98-100.

51 *Ibid.*, 106-7.

52 *Ibid.*, 108.

53 *Ibid.*, 110.

54 *Ibid.*, 111.

55 *Ibid.*, 112.

56 *Ibid.*, 114.

57 *Ibid.*, 115.

58 *Ibid.*

59 *Ibid.*, 116.

60 *Ibid.*

61 *Ibid.*, 117.

62 Cited in C. S. Lewis, *Surprised by Joy* (New York: Harcourt Brace Jovanovich, 1955), 212.

63 *Ibid.*, 118.

64 *Ibid.*, 118-19.

65 In some branches of contemporary theology, hell is rationalized from reality. John Hick is a good example of such thinking when he refers to hell in his work, *Evil and the God of Love*, as a "grim fantasy" (p. 385). Although Hick provides a fine summary of the major issues and history concerning the problem of evil, his "soul building" theology resorts to universalism as a solution to the problem of evil (p. 381). However, universalism is just "sanctified" determinism. If all men will eventually end up in heaven, then their choices, be they good or evil,

make no significant difference. Hence, universalism, like determinism, reduces the importance of free will. [John Hick, *Evil and the God of Love* (London: Macmillan, 1966.)]

66   *Ibid.*, 121.
67   *Ibid.*
68   *Ibid.*, 122.
69   *Ibid.*, 124.
70   *Ibid.*, 126.
71   *Ibid.*
72   *Ibid.*, 127-28.
73   *Ibid.*, 128.
74   *Ibid.*, 133.
75   *Ibid.*, 133-36.
76   *Ibid.*, 137
77   *Ibid.*, 144.
78   *Ibid.*, 148.
79   Wall, *op. cit.*, 448.
80   C. S. Lewis, *A Grief Observed* (New York: Bantam Books, 1961), 1.
81   *Ibid.*, 4-5.
82   *Ibid.*, 5.
83   *Ibid.*, 15.
84   *Ibid.*, 25.
85   *Ibid.*, 31.
86   *Ibid.*, 33-35
87   *Ibid.*, 46-47.
88   *Ibid.*, 45-47.
89   *Ibid.*, 50.
90   *Ibid.*, 61.
91   *Ibid.*, 76-77.
92   *Ibid.*, 80-81.
93   Robert H. Smith, *Patches of Godlight* (Athens, GA: University of Georgia Press, 1981), 223.
94   Talmage C. Johnson, "The Meaning and Use of Pain," review of *The Problem of Pain* by C. S. Lewis, *Christian Century*, 1 December 1943, 1400.
95   C. E. M. Joad, "The Pains of Animals: A Problem in Theology," review of *The Problem of Pain* by C. S. Lewis, *Atlantic Monthly*, August 1950, 57.
96   See C. E. M. Joad, *God and Evil* (Freeport, NY: Books for Libraries, 1943).
97   See Michael, D. Meschiliman, *The Restitution of Man: C. S. Lewis and the Case Against Scientism* (Grand Rapids, MI: William B. Eerdmans, 1983.

98   Tom Driberg, "Lobbies of the Soul," *New Statesman and Nation* XLIX (March 19, 1955), 393-94, cited in Richard B. Cunningham, *C. S. Lewis: Defender of the Faith* (Philadelphia: Westminster, 1967), 15.

99   Richard B. Cunningham, *C. S. Lewis: Defender of the Faith* (Philadelphia: Westminster, 1967), 114.

100   Kathryn Lindskoog, *C. S. Lewis: Mere Christian* (Downers Grove, IL: InterVarsity, 1981), 134.

101   Joad, *op. cit.*, 58.

102   *Ibid.*

103   *Ibid.*

104   Wall, *op. cit.*, 450-51.

CONCLUSION

What Must We Conclude?

In the preceding six chapters, we have seen that the problem of evil from a historical, biblical, theological, philosophical, and human perspective is complicated and demanding. Humankind, in the present and in the future, will continue to wrestle with this issue. Yet the difficulty and depth of this problem is by no means an excuse to "modify" our concept of an infinite, personal God who is deeply involved with both the experiential and historical implications of suffering. Human suffering constitutes both a problem and a promise. All too often, the magnitude of the problem takes precedence over the promise. This promise, rooted in the biblical position of the Judeo-Christian worldview, supplies a suffering Savior, a redeeming Christ, a resurrected Lord, and a reigning King and Prince of Peace that will one day return to usher in a new heaven and a new earth.

In chapter 1, we noted that the demonic not only involves the abuse of free will; demonic activity is also substantiated by both scripture and branches of modern psychological and medical opinion. And yet, because scripture is silent regarding some of the hows and whys of the origin of evil, we too must be silent. "I don't know" is often a better answer than dogmatic speculation concerning evil. The Bible, although true, does not reveal the entire mind of God; thus God, in His infinite wisdom, gave us intended silence rather than all the answers to our present life. In the context of fallen man, some of the answers could be far wiser than all the answers.

In chapter 2, part 1, we noted that mankind has two options for altering both environment and personality: either the attempt to "change" humankind from the inside or from the outside. As we concluded, to change humankind from the outside is merely treating the socioeconomic symptom rather than the sinful and fallen cause. The roots and not the "branches" of humankind produce the greatest growth of evil.

However, in chapter 2, part 2, the biblical appraisal of human nature brought us both reality and hope. Man is fallen yet is of infinite value because he is endowed with the image of God. For humankind to solve the problem of his or her own evil, humans must first solve the problem of their own sinfulness. Redemption through Christ thus provides humans with the possibility of a new nature and a new hope.

A consistent theme (which ran through all six chapters) was free will. Free will, as opposed to a robot-determinism, is the strongest apologetic weapon one can deploy for an offensive (rather than defensive) treatment of evil. If human will is by definition free, then that will is self-caused; thus humans are responsible for their choices and the consequences of those choices. But if human will is predetermined before he or she makes a choice, the result is a human "robot" that responds without responsibility. Predestination, a topic that theologians have debated for centuries, may shed light concerning matters of salvation, but it is of limited help to the nonbeliever. The cause of evil may rest in humankind's independent choice rather than a deterministic "mold." To end all evil, God would therefore have to violate free will or eliminate free will entirely.

One of the greatest illustrations of suffering, Job, showed us the mystery and the lessons of suffering. It is essential to remember that as we read Job, we can understand more of his trials than Job himself did. We have the script after the completed play. Job had only his experience without the aid of God's written revelation. If Job could only read his "biography" now, one wonders what he would conclude. The chapter on Job taught us the value of hindsight as compared to foresight.

In chapter 5, we observed the need for accurate semantics and logic as one approaches the problem of evil. Ironically, the nontheist or atheist often commits the same logical fallacies he or she attempts to refute. Furthermore, some nontheists also attempt to navigate with foggy, rather than theologically clear, definitions regarding the attributes of God. There are things God cannot do (e.g., lie), but these limitations concern His nature, not His omnipotence. Uncritical absorption of "weak" theology and critical thinking often leads to false conclusions.

As for chapter 6, one should note that C. S. Lewis utilizes the preceding arguments to support biblical Christianity. He asserted the reality of Satan, the Fall of man, the hindsight of Job, the cure of redemption, the logical validity of Christianity, and the grief of his own experience with pain. Lewis supplies the most effective arguments to bolster the strength of biblical Christianity. In fact, Lewis was himself an atheist for half of his life—until the compelling evidence for the truth of Christianity turned him to faith in Christ. Lewis was not immune to the grief and reality of suffering. Through being wounded in war, facing various and serious illnesses, and the loss of his wife to cancer, Lewis was a scholar who both understood and felt pain. Lewis thus provides a helpful synthesis of the needed ingredients to accurately deal with evil, pain, and suffering.

Finally, the redemption of Christ, as discussed in chapter 4, brings us to the brutal yet wonderous solution to pain and evil. If it were not for the cross, the problem of evil would indeed be a problem. A cure has arisen from outside the human situation from One who became a part of the human situation. God became man in Christ, suffered, died, and rose again from the dead so that man may one day never suffer. Christ arose from the dead so that man's greatest enemy (death), may forever be a means and not an end of suffering.

I don't have all the answers to suffering. I do know this: something happened over two thousand years ago, in time and space, witnessed by over five hundred people, that changed human history. It changed me. I have experienced the personal, historical, intellectual, and risen Christ. Do I still have Tourette's? Yes, I do, and I have it for His glory, not mine.

Jesus said in John 14:6 (NASB): "I am the way, and the truth, and the life; no one comes to the Father but through Me." Because of our *choice* against Him, God, due to moral necessity, will not promise us a life immune from suffering and pain. The consequences of the Fall, although vast, are not such that God would ignore them by violating humankind's free will. Despite the reality of suffering, God has indeed promised the following hope for those who choose Christ: a *way* to endure suffering, a *truth* to understand suffering, and everlasting *life* to forever eliminate suffering.

BIBLIOGRAPHY

Books

Achilles, Ernst. "Evil, Bad, Wickedness." *The New International Dictionary of New Testament Theology*. Vol. 1. Ed. Colin Brown. Grand Rapids, MI: Zondervan, 1967.

Andersen, Francis I. *Job: An Introduction and Commentary. Tyndale Old Testament Commentaries*. Vol. 13. Ed. D. J. Wiseman. Downers Grove, IL: InterVarsity, 1976.

Aquinas, Thomas. *Introduction to Saint Thomas Aquinas*. Ed. Anton C. Pegis. New York: Random House, 1948.

Archer, Gleason. *A Survey of Old Testament Introduction*. Chicago: Moody, 1979.

———. *Encyclopedia of Biblical Difficulties*. Chicago: Moody, 1982.

———. *Problem of Underserved Suffering*. Grand Rapids, MI, 1982.

Arndt, William, and Wilbur F. Gingrich. *A Greek English Lexicon of the New Testament and Other Early Christian Literature*. Chicago: University of Chicago Press, 1979.

Augustine, *The City of God*. Trans. Gerald G. Walsh, Demetrius B. Zema, Grace Monahan, and Daniel J. Honan. Garden City, NY: Image Books, 1958.

Barth, Karl. *Church Dogmatics: The Doctrine of Creation.* Vol. 3. Eds. G.W. Bromiley and T.F. Torrance. Edinburgh; T. and T. Clark, 1960.

Beller, E. and Lee M. Jr., eds. *Selections from Bayle's Dictionary.* Princeton: Princeton University Press, 1952.

Bietenhard, H. "Satan, Beelzebel, Devil, Exorcism." *The International Dictionary of New Testament Theology.* Vol. 3. Ed. Colin Brown. Grand Rapids, MI: Zondervan, 1979.

Blum, Jerome, Rondo Cameron, and Thomas G. Barnes, *A History: The European World.* Boston: Little, Brown, 1966.

Bode, William. *The Book of Job and the Solution of the Problem of Suffering It Offers.* Grand Rapids, MI: Eerdmans, 1914.

Brinton, Crane. "Enlightenment." *The Encyclopedia of Philosophy.* Vol. 2. Ed. Paul Edwards. New York: Macmillan and Free Press, 1967.

Brown, Colin. "Redemption." *The New International Dictionary of New Testament Theology.* Vol. 3. Ed. Colin Brown. Grand Rapids, MI: Zondervan, 1971.

Bruce, F.F. *The New Testament Documents: Are They Reliable?* Downers Grove, IL: InterVarsity, 1982.

Burrows, Millar. *An Outline of Biblical Theology.* Philadelphia: Westminster, 1946.

Carnell, Edward John. *An Introduction of Christian Apologetics.* Grand Rapids, MI: Eerdmans, 1948.

Clark, E.D. *The Universe: Plan or Accident?* Philadelphia: Muhlenburg, 1961.

Copi, Irving M. *Introduction to Logic.* New York: Macmillan, 1982.

Copleston, Fredrick J. *A History of Philosophy*. Vol. 1. Part 2. *Greece and Rome*. Garden City, NY: Image Books, 1962.

———. *A History of Philosophy*. Vol. 9. Part 1. *Maine de Biran to Sartre*. Garden City, NY: Image Books, 1974.

———. *A History of Philosophy*. Vol. 2. Part 2. *Mediaeval Philosophy*. Garden City, NY: Image Books, 1962.

Cunningham, Richard B. *Defender of the Faith*. Philadelphia: Westminster, 1967.

Danto, Arthur C. "Naturalism." *The Encyclopedia of Philosophy*. Vol. 5. Ed. Paul Edwards. New York: Macmillan and Free Press, 1967.

Delitzsch, Franz Julius. *A New Commentary on Genesis*. Vol. 1. Trans. Sophia Taylor. London: T. and T. Clark, 1888.

Diniger, Simon. *A Theology for Modern Man: The Nature of Man in Theological and Psychological Perspective*. New York: Harper and Brother, 1962.

Donnelly, John, ed. *Logical Analysis and Contemporary Theism*. New York: Fordham University Press, 1972.

Dostoevsky, Fydor M. *The Brothers Karamazov*. Trans. Andrew H. MacAndrew. Toronto: Bantam Books, 1970.

Ducasse, H.J. *A Philosophical Scrutiny of Religion*. New York, 1953.

Edersheim, Alfred. *O.T. Bible History*. Vol. 1. 1909 reprint. Grand Rapids, MI: William B Eerdmans, 1979.

Ellul, Jacques. *Perspectives on Our Age*. Trans. Joachim Neugroschel. New York: Seabury, 1981.

Farrar, Fredrick. *The Life of Christ*. Dutton: Cassel and Co., 1897.

Feinberg, John Samuel. *The Literary and Theological Implications of the Prologue and Epilogue of Job.* MA thesis, Talbot Theological Seminary, 1971.

Ferguson, John. *Pelagius.* Cambridge: W. Heffer and Sons, 1956.

Flew and Macintyre, eds. *Theology and Falsification.* New York, 1955.

Freud, Sigmund. *Two Short Accounts of Psycho-Analysis.* Trans. and ed. James Strachey. London: Penguin Books, 1962.

Geisler, Norman. *Christian Apologetics.* Grand Rapids, MI: Baker Book, 1976

———. *Inerrancy.* Grand Rapids, MI: Zondervan, 1979.

———. *Is Man the Measure?* Grand Rapids, MI: Baker Book House, 1983.

———. *Philosophy of Religion.* Grand Rapids, MI: Zondervan, 1974.

———. *The Roots of Evil.* Grand Rapids, MI: Zondervan, 1978.

Genung, John F. "Job." *The International Standard Bible Encyclopedia.* Vol. 3. Ed. James Orr. Grand Rapids, MI: William B. Eerdmans, 1939.

Gilbert, Neal W. "Renaissance." *The Encyclopedia of Philosophy.* Vol. 7. Ed. Paul Edwards. New York: Macmillan, 1967.

Gordis, Robert. *The Book of God and Man; A Study of Job.* Chicago: University of Chicago Press, 1965.

Green, Michael. *I Believe in Satan's Downfall.* Grand Rapids, MI: William B. Eerdmans, 1981.

Guttmann, Julius. *Philosophies of Judaism.* New York: Schocken Books, 1973.

Haley, John W. *Alleged Discrepancies of the Bible*. 1874. Reprint. Grand Rapids, MI: Baker Book, 1977.

Harris, Laird R., Gleason L. Archer, and Bruce K. Waltke eds. *Theological Wordbook of the Old Testament*. 2 vols. Chicago: Moody, 1980.

Harrison, R.K. *Introduction to the Old Testament*. Grand Rapids, MI: William B. Eerdmans, 1969.

Hengel, Martin. *Crucifixion*. Philadelphia: Fortress Press, 1977.

Henry, Carl F.H. ed. *Basic Christian Doctrines*. Grand Rapids, MI: Baker Book, 1962.

———. *Christian Personal Ethics*. Grand Rapids, MI: Baker Book House, 1957.

———. *God, Revelation, and Authority*. Vol. 6. Waco, TX: Word Books, 1983.

———. (ed.). *Horizons of Science*. New York: Harper and Row, 1977.

Hick, John. *Evil and the God of Love*. London: Macmillan, 1966.

———. *Theology and Verification: The Existence of God*. New York: Macmillan, 1964.

Hopkins, Hugh A.E. *The Mystery of Suffering*. Chicago: InterVarsity Press, 1959.

Humanist Manifesto. Vols. 1 and 2. Buffalo, NY: Prometheus, 1976.

Jensen, Irving L. *Syllabus*. Bib. 203. Columbia Bible College, 1980.

Joad, C. E. M. *God and Evil*. Freeport, NY: Books for Libraries, 1943.

Jurgens, William A. ed. *The Faith of the Early Fathers*. 3 vols. Collegeville, MN: Liturgical Press, 1970.

Kahane, Howard. *Logic and Philosophy: A Modern Introduction*. Belmont, CA: Wadsworth, 1982.

Kahn, Steven ed. *Classics in Western Philosophy*. Indianapolis, IN: Hackett, 1977.

Kallas, James. *The Real Satan: From Biblical Times to Present*. Minneapolis, MN: Augsburg, 1975.

Kenyon, Fredrick G. *The Bible and Archaeology*. New York: Harper and Row,1940.

King, A. R. *The Problem of Evil*. New York: Ronald Press, 1952.

Kitamori, Kazoh. *Theology of the Pain of God*. Richmond, VA: John Knox, 1965.

Kofahl, Robert E. and Kelly L. Segraves. *The Creation Explanation: A Scientific Alternative to Evolution*. Wheaton, IL: Harold Shaw, 1975.

Koop, C. Everett, and Francis A. Schaeffer. *Whatever Happened to the Human Race?* Westchester, IL: Crossway Books, 1979.

Kraeling, Emil G. *The Book of the Ways of God*. New York: Charles Scribner and Sons, 1938.

Laidlow, John. *The Biblical Doctrine of Man*. Edinburgh: T. and T. Clark, 1895.

Lewis, C. S. *A Grief Observed*. Toronto: Bantam Books, 1961.

———. *Surprised by Joy*. New York: Harcourt Brace and Jovanovich, 1955.

————. *Christian Reflections*. Ed. Walter Hooper. Grand Rapids, MI: 1967.

————. *The Problem of Pain*. New York: Macmillan, 1962.

Lindskoog, Kathryn. *C.S. Lewis: Mere Christian*. Downers Grove, IL: InterVarsity, 1981.

Lorenz, Konrad Z. *On Aggression*. Trans. Marjorie Latzke. London: Muthuen University Paperback, 1966.

Luther, Martin. *Luther's Commentary on Genesis* Trans. J. Theodore Mueller. Grand Rapids, MI: Zondervan, 1958.

Machaelis, Wilhelm. "Pascho." *Theological Dictionary of the New Testament*. Vol. 5. Ed. Gerhard Kittel. Trans. and ed. Geoffrey W. Bromiley. Grand Rapids, MI: William B. Eerdmans, 1967.

Machen, J.G. *Christianity and Liberalism*. Grand Rapids, MI: Eerdmans, 1923.

Mallow, Vernon R. *The Demonic: An Examination into the Theology of Edwin Lewis, Karl Barth, and Paul Tillich*. Lanham, MD: University Press of America, 1983.

Marx, Karl. *Karl Marx: Selected Writings in Sociology and Social Philosophy*. Trans. T. B. Bottomore. Eds. T. B. Bottomore and M. Rubel. London: Penguin Books, 1963.

McDowell, Josh. *Evidence That Demands a Verdict: Historical Evidences for the Christian Faith*. San Bernardino, CA: Here's Life Publishers, 1972.

Mctaggart, J. E. *Some Dogmas of Religion*. London, 1906.

Meschiliman, Michael D. *The Restitution of Man: C.S. Lewis and the Case Against Scientism*. Grand Rapids, MI: William B. Eerdmans, 1983.

Mill, John Stuart. *The Utility of Religion*. New York, 1957.

Milton, John. *Paradise Lost*. Ed. Rob Vaughn. London: Cassel, Petter, and Galpin, 1866.

Montgomery, John Warwick. *Crisis in Lutheran Theology*. Grand Rapids, MI: William B. Eerdmans, 1967.

———. *Demon Possession: A Medical, Historical, Anthropological, and Theological Symposium*. Minneapolis, MN: Bethany House, 1976.

———. *God's Inerrant Word: An International Symposium*. Minneapolis, MN: Bethany House, 1974.

———. *Faith Founded on Fact*. Nashville, TN: Thomas Nelson, 1978.

———. *The Quest for Noah's Ark*. 2d rev. ed. Minneapolis, MN: Bethany House, 1974.

———. *Jurisprudence: A Book of Readings*. 2nd ed. Strasbourg, France: International Scholarly Publishers, 1974.

———. *The Shaping of America*. Minneapolis, MN: Bethany House, 1976.

———. *The Shape of the Past*. 2d rev. ed. Minneapolis, MN: Bethany House, 1975.

Morris, Leon. *The Apostolic Preaching of the Cross*. Grand Rapids, MI: William B. Eerdmans, 1955.

Murray, John. *The Epistle to. the Romans. The New International Commentary on the New Testament*. Vols. 1 and 2. Ed. F. F. Bruce. Grand Rapids, MI: William B. Eerdmans, 1959.

Niebuhr, Reinhold. *The Nature and Destiny of Man: A Christian Interpretation*. London: Nisbet, 1941.

Pearce, Victor E. K. *Who Was Adam?* Great Britain: Paternoster Press, 1969.

Peterson, Michael. *Evil and the Christian God*. Grand Rapids, MI: Baker Book, 1982.

Pfeiffer, Charles F., and Everett F. Harrison eds. *The Wycliffe Bible Commentary*. Chicago: Moody Press, 1962.

Plantinga, Alvin. *God and Other Minds*. New York: Cornell University Press, 1967.

———. *God, Freedom, and Evil*. Grand Rapids, MI: William B. Eerdmans, 1980.

———. *The Nature of Necessity*. New York: Oxford University Press, 1974.

Plato, *The Republic*. Trans. H.D.P. Lee. London: Penguin Books, 1955.

Sartre, Jean-Paul. *Existentialism and Human Emotions*. New York: Philosophical Library, 1957.

Schaff, Phillip ed. *History of The Christian Church*. 8 vols. Grand Rapids, MI: William B. Eerdmans, 1910.

Shakespeare, William. *Hamlet*. Ed. E. K. Chambers. Boston: D. C. Heath, 1893.

Skinner, B. F. *Science and Human Behavior*. New York: Macmillan, 1953.

Smith, Robert H. *Patches of Godlight*. Athens GA: University of Georgia Press, 1981.

Sontag, Fredrick. *The God of Evil: An Argument from the Existence of the Devil*. New York: Harper and Row, 1970.

Standen, Anthony. *Science Is a Sacred Cow*. New York: E. P. Dutton, 1950.

Stevenson, Leslie. *Seven Theories of Human Nature*. New York: Oxford University Press, 1974.

Tennant, F. R. *The Sources of the Doctrines of the Fall and Original Sin*. Cambridge: at the University Press, 1974.

Tenney, Merrill C. ed. *The Bible: The Living Word of God*. Grand Rapids, MI: Zondervan, 1968.

Thiessen, Henry Clarence. *Lectures in Systematic Theology*. Grand Rapids, MI: William B. Eerdmans, 1955.

Venable, Vernon. *Human Nature: The Marxian View*. New York: Alfred A. Knopf, 1946.

Warfield, Benjamin B. *The Inspiration and Authority of the Bible*. Phillipsburg, NJ: Presbyterian and Reformed Publishing, 1948.

———. "The Person of Christ." *The International Standard Bible Encyclopedia*. Vol. 4. Ed. James Orr. Grand Rapids, MI: William B. Eerdmans, 1939.

———. *The Person and Work of Christ*. Ed. Samuel G. Craig. Phillipsburg, NJ: Presbyterian and Reformed Publishing, 1950.

Websters New World Dictionary of the American Language. New York: World, 1970.

Wenham, John M. *The Goodness of God*. Downers Grove, IL: InterVarsity, 1974.

Wilder-Smith, A. E. *Man's Origin, Man's Destiny*. Wheaton, IL: Harold Shaw, 1969.

Wingren, Gustaf. *Theology in Conflict*. Trans. Eric H. Wahlstrom. Philadelphia: Muhlenberg Press, 1958.

Wysong, R. L. *The Creation-Evolution Controversy.* Midlands, MI: Inquiry, 1976.

Journals and Periodicals

Aiken, Henry D. "God and Evil: A Study of Some Relations Between Faith and Morals." *Ethics* 68 (1958): 77-97.

Davis, Truman C. "The Crucifixion of Jesus: The Passion of Christ from a Medical Point of View." *Arizona Medicine* (March 1965): 183-87.

Driberg, Tom. "Lobbies of the Soul." *New Statesman and Nation* 49 (March 19, 1955): 393-94.

Fingarette, Herbert. "The Meaning of Law in the Book of Job." *Hastings Law Journal* 29, no. 6 (July 1978): 1581-1617.

Geisler, Norman. "Man's Destiny: Free or Forced?" *Christian Scholar's Review* 9, no. 2, (1979): 99-109.

Hayman, A. P. "Rabbinic Judaism and the Problem of Evil." *Scottish Journal of Theology* 29, no. 5 (1976): 461-76.

Jaffa, Henry V. "An Enduring Legacy of Error." *The Register.* (March 16, 1983): A19.

Joad, C. E. M. "The Pains of Animals." *Atlantic Monthly.* (August 1950), 57-59.

Johnson, Talmage C. "The Meaning and Use of Pain." *Christian Century* 60 (December 1943): 1400.

Livingstone, David N. "Evolution as Metaphor and Myth." *Christian Scholars Review* 7, no. 2, (1983): 111-25.

Mackie, J. L. "Evil and Omnipotence." *Mind* 64 (1955): 200-212.

McCloskey, H. J. "God and Evil." *Philosophical Quarterly* 10 (1960): 96-114.

Montgomery, John Warwick. "The Marxist Approach to Human Rights." *Simon Greenleaf Law Review* 3 (1983-84): 7-183.

Samenow, Stanton E. "The Criminal Personality: New Concepts and New Procedures for Change." *Humanist* (Sept./Oct. 1978): 16-19.

Solzenitsen, Alexander. "A World Split Apart." *National Review* (July 7, 1978), 836-55.

Wall, Robert. "The Problem of Observed Suffering." *Journal of the Evangelical Theological Society* 26, no. 4 (December 1983): 443-51.

Walls, Jerry. "The Free Will Defense." *Christian Scholars Review* 8, no. 1 (1983): 19-33.

APPENDIX

A Cross in an Ocean Voyage

There is a pleasure in the pathless woods,
There is a rapture on a lonely shore,
There is society where no one intrudes by the deep sea,
and music in its roar:
I love not man the less, but nature more,
From these our interviews, in which I steal from all I may
be, or have been before,
To mingle with the universe, and feel
What I can ne'er express, yet cannot all conceal...

As I arose from my bed midway through a calm, soft night along the Florida coast, little did I know that tonight my life was to begin an inward metamorphosis, a metamorphosis of heart and soul. Why I woke at such an odd hour, I do not know, but this I know, like a magnet I was drawn to the ocean. I quietly dressed, then embarked on a short walk to the shore just two hundred yards away. The closer I came to the call of these waves, the closer I felt to something or someone, but what or who it was, I did not know. When I reached the sand, I sat down about twenty yards from this massive, dark aquatic mirror that reflected power unmatched in nature's revelation. As I gazed and felt the awesome power and hidden beauty of the ocean, I was filled with puzzled contentment. I knew something, someone beyond just a pantheistic expression of nature was present, but who? The depths of my heart desired to speak, yet who would listen? In spite of this seemingly nonexistent dialogue that I so desired, I softly spoke. I cried out in silent passion; was I heard?

The preceding encounter with the ocean was but one stop amidst the many voyages my life had taken and would take as I drifted in search of truth.

It was the summer and the freedom mixed with it after ninth grade that instigated my trip to Florida. Being older than the average ninth-grader, I had proudly received my driver's license in January of that year. Thus, a two-week pilgrimage down to Florida was quite appropriate for myself and two older high school buddies. So, we loaded up our Ford '67 Galaxy 500 with a strong desire for girl watching, partying, and many other desires that might enhance our trip, then we took off.

The following two weeks were fun, but in reality, they were empty.

Apart from my midnight encounter with the ocean, I returned home to Indianapolis just as fulfilled and happy, yet ironically as empty as when I had left. This trip was no different from any other prior voyage that my life had sought to find meaning for myself.

The most painful voyage of my life was during early grade school. Those years were hard because my intellectual self-image was severely marred during this time. In fact, the memories of first grade are still as vivid as if they happened yesterday. On one specific instance during first grade, I can remember the damage that my teacher, Mrs. McClain, inflicted upon my young mind. Mrs. McClain was in the process of organizing her class, and I made an honest mistake by going to the wrong table. When she noticed my mistake,

I was quickly introduced to her little stuffed monkey. This monkey represented a symbol of failure, for when a student blundered in some way, he or she had to wear this monkey's hat around for all to see. The hat was more than just a comic reminder that you were "dumb"; it was more so a knife wound to my five-year-old self-image. In addition, Mrs. McClain also wanted her students reading on a third-grade level by the end of first grade. But if you failed to meet this standard, further ridicule was endorsed upon you.

For instance, I recall one incident in which Mrs. McClain lined up the whole class in a row, then she preceded to ask each student how many books he or she had read. If your quota of books was to her satisfaction, you were rewarded with a smile and a pat on the back. And if you had not read enough books, she would look at you in disgust and say, "Blaaaa, that's no good!" It was not that I did not try or lacked the needed ability to learn, but instead I lacked the needed support and patience of my teacher. Mrs. McClain's continued attacks on my lack of performance destroyed my desire to learn.

As my grade school years advanced, this painful intellectual self-image problem advanced with me. Second grade, third grade, fourth grade, etc., were painful and frustrating years due to such a poor first-grade foundation. In fact, I was so ashamed and scared when report cards were issued, I would lie to my friends about my grades to hide my shame. Society's academic label on my life was nothing but Cs, Ds, and Fs. Without the passionate concern and care of my mother, I never would have made it through school. She sought the needed private tutors in English and math, and she also made sure I attended summer school sessions. She even instigated one of the most important educational reforms, for which I am overwhelmingly grateful: I was to repeat the fifth grade.

These painful waves were beginning to settle now. The sea was unsure yet calm, and my painful drifting began to emerge into a purposeful course of success.

With these difficult experiences behind me, plus the added maturity from my repetition of the fifth grade, my next voyage in life traveled in a ship called success. This success was anchored in athletics. I had always possessed a natural athletic ability, yet it did not surface until my sixth-grade preparation for field day. This field day, a one-day event every spring, consisted of solid competition in events such as the triple jump, high jump, shot put, long distance running, and relays. As I prepared for this event, my two choices of competition consisted of the triple jump and the shot put. Thus, with committed dedication I practiced and prepared my athletic frame for a challenging round of track and field events. When field day arrived, I was confident that a first in the shot put event would be no problem, and it was not. But in the triple jump, a strong, stocky, and confident Jewish boy, who was my best friend, would be an easy opponent to rob me of my quest for victory. When the event was finished, I had defeated my friend Bruce by one inch with a jump of thirty feet. Two blue ribbons and the honor and recognition that came with them were mine. I was beginning to become someone.

After finishing the sixth grade, I was soon to attend a school through which success in my life would continue to spread. The name of this school was Westlane Junior High. It was here that I became one of the most popular and respected students in the student body. This popularity and respect emerged because of my continued athletic, musical, and social achievements. I was the first-string quarterback on our football team two years in a row. I also became the first seventh-grader to letter in golf and later was awarded the most valuable player award in this sport. Furthermore,

I had also been taking private drum lessons since fifth grade, so by the time auditions for concert band, stage band, and orchestra came, I easily obtained first or second chair in the percussion section. In addition, I was elected to a number of student representative positions through which I received substantial recognition from my peers. The natural by-product of all the above accomplishments was also an excellent magnet to draw the attention of Westlane's female constituency.

In essence, I had everything that any junior high student would love to call his own. I had popularity, talent, good looks, a loving family, tons of friends, and respect from all. However, during February of seventh grade, a dark and awesome storm cloud was approaching my life that would release a difficult yet essential lightning bolt of despair upon my life. Although this storm caused little outward change in my social and athletic endeavors, deep inside it transformed my insight into the bluntness of life's cold realities. The striving to fulfill the middle-class image of the successful all-American boy vanished with the sudden terror that was to strike my life.

The day included the average events in the life of a seventh-grader. It was Thursday morning, and I rose from bed, dressed, and brushed my teeth. I then proceeded to have my daily morning rendezvous with my father at the breakfast table.

The past few months my father had been rising early to fix my breakfast. My mother had just arrived home from the hospital. She was still gaining her strength from an operation through which half of her stomach was removed. In fact, at one time her condition was so severe that death almost conquered this noble woman. In spite of this, she pulled through and was well on the way to recovery.

These consistent, small acts of kindness from my father were showered upon my life from early childhood on. He was a kind, gentle, and compassionate man that had no inhibitions toward loving his wife and three kids. I can still feel the warmth of his hands upon mine when I would absorb myself in his secure lap, during which I would hear his voice meet my ear with the words, "I love you."

As I finished my breakfast on that Thursday morning, my father showed me one or two of his old wrestling medals for encouragement. Today I had a wrestling meet after school. When I completed my early-morning feast, I gathered my things and said goodbye. Yet I did not know that I would never again sit at the breakfast table with my father—that afternoon my father died at home.

His death was such a shock that it almost seemed like a dream. However, the dream soon ended when I stood before the open coffin of the one I had loved so; one whose body and life was now quiet, still, cold, and lifeless. The warmth of his hands were now only memories.

I will never erase from my mind my father's funeral service just prior to his burial. As I sat in the front row of that breathtaking and beautiful Episcopal church that I had attended for most of my young life, I recall his silver coffin draped in purple buntings. I stared at his coffin; thoughts were racing through my mind at a deep and emotional speed. Near the end of the service, his casket was slowly wheeling down the long isle of the sanctuary.

As my father passed my pew, I rose and followed in what seemed to be the most difficult walking voyage of my life. With his casket rolling before me, and at least five hundred people gazing at this quiet procession of father and son, a flood of tears, emotion, and sorrow overcame me as I walked. It was the last walk my father and I would take together.

My heart was now soft, and my life was ready for its most crucial voyage.

The church I attended struck me as a distant building in which people would gather to become an ecclesiastical country club of "good" people. My presupposition was that it was someplace you had to go. It struck me as an arena of forced obligation that made you feel better if you attended and guilty if you did not. If fact, I hated to go to church. Church was boring. Church was useless. I even remember one Sunday morning when I cried, pleaded, and begged with my parents in a futile attempt to avoid this Sunday prison that pinned me to a pew, sung me to sleep, and prayed me to boredom. My pleading did little good, for I still had to go.

Later, I was enrolled in confirmation class, memorized a few creeds, listened to a few ecclesiastical facts, and then was blessed by some famous bishop during my confirmation service. To me, it all seemed to be just acts of empty ritualism through which I could feel guilt free. Where was the meaning behind all this ritual and form? The external image of the church left me empty and puzzled, while my internal heart was desperately seeking someone or something. Hence, my problem was not with a real God, for I believed He existed, but instead my problem lay in the unreal externals of the church. I wanted more than just ritual and tradition—I wanted a person. As a result, I adopted my own simple and common philosophy of a ticket to heaven that went as follows: If I do more good things than bad, I will go to heaven.

Yet little did I know that this philosophy was just as empty and false as the external ritualism that I so detested.

Although my quick readjustment to a normal life after my father's death, compounded with my "be good" philosophy, seemed to satisfy for a short while, I soon began to thirst more for the depths of a meaningful existence. In eighth and ninth grade, experimentation with pot, alcohol, partying, etc., soon led me to see that this all-American boy owned internal evil desires that left me very uncomfortable. Even though I was basically a nice guy, I still saw drives and actions in myself that painted my conscience with guilt and shame. I felt incomplete even though I had all I wanted. I had everything, yet nothing. I was drowning in a sea of existential "goodness."

Consequently, this preceding thirst for deeper meaning led me to an intellectual pursuit for truth. How ironic it was that the area of my life that haunted me so during first grade would now be the tool to lead me toward truth. Thus, in ninth grade I began to read and read. I did not read just anything but instead plunged my mind into books such as *Lord of the Flies*, *The Exorcist*, *When to Say Hello*, and *I'm OK You're OK*. Despite the input from these novels and self-improvement books, I soon found out that I was not okay! In addition, I had always respected the Bible, at least what little I knew of it, so I embarked on a reading of this book. Like any other book, I started at the beginning, but I could not see how creation, Adam and Eve, and Noah applied to my situation. Thus, I stopped reading the Bible, not for lack of interest, but for lack of understanding.

However, one of my best friends was given a copy of the Living Bible by his grandmother. During the many times that I thumbed through this Bible, I found some chapters that spoke a language my empty heart could hear. These chapters were the Sermon on the Mount. I could not evade the truth, wisdom, and warmth of this man called Jesus. Indeed, this man Jesus seemed to speak truth, whereas everyone and everything else was just words. But how was this passage and Jesus's life to affect me? I was dying to understand. How I longed for someone to explain.

In retrospect, it was the preceding voyages from childhood to age sixteen that led me to my midnight encounter on the Florida coast. Yet after returning from Florida to begin my sophomore year of high school, my endless voyages would soon end. This someone behind the ocean was preparing to answer my cry. Our never-ending dialogue was soon to begin.

It was Friday night, and my best friend Chris Miller and I were at a party. Chris told me of a meeting that was starting later that night, and he persistently mentioned that we should attend. After a few more attempts at persuading me, we climbed in the car and drove to the Nora Teen Barn. However, completely foreign to my knowledge, Chris had himself discovered one week earlier who this someone behind the ocean was.

This building, the Nora Teen Barn, was actually an old barn that had been renovated to accommodate youth meetings. When we arrived, there was a large group of about two hundred high school students gathered. Chris and I sat down on the floor in expectation for the meeting to start.

The meeting began with everybody singing songs about Jesus, yet I began to notice something different about the message of these songs. After two or three songs, a man came to the front and began to explain the uniqueness of the Bible, but he did not stop there. Instead, he went beyond just the uniqueness and the story of the Bible, for the main character of this book was Jesus Christ. As he spoke and clearly explained this thing called the gospel, my heart and mind were glued to every word.

At the end of his message, I knew my final yet beginning voyage was before me. That someone I had so sincerely cried for on that Florida beach had a name, an identity. He was Jehovah, God, the Lord Jesus Christ. Hence, at that moment on October 12, 1974, around 9:30 p.m., while drowning in a meaningless ocean of endless searching, I pushed aside the sinking debris of my self-image, my success, my pride, and my "goodness," and desperately clung to the only truth that would end my voyage: a blood-stained cross floating in the sea of eternity.

Stuart Atkins

Thou glorious mirror, where the Almighty's form Glasses itself in tempests; in all time,
Calm or convulsed, in breeze, or gale, or storm,
Icing the pole, or in the torrid clime Dark-heaving; boundless, endless, and sublime, The image of Eternity, the throne.

—George Gordon Byron

6/7/91

Dear Steve,

Over the past year and a half, I am confident you, as anyone would, have struggled with the balance between reality and optimism. Perhaps you have fought numerous emotions such as fear, joy, resentment, guilt, bitterness, despair, and just the perplexity of the unknown. I know that if I were faced with the current battle you are waging, life at times would seem like a never-ending staircase that rises with each step. The things that we so often take for granted in life have become your treasures, because oddly enough, suffering uncovers the true meaning of things we never thought or took the time to see as meaningful.

Whether you encounter a full and complete recovery or face the realities of life after life, I wish with the utmost of respect and sincerity to return a favor your way. Perhaps you will remember my call to you two years ago asking for advice concerning programming languages. I asked out of all the languages available, which do you feel would combine both simplicity, adaptability, and power combined into one language. Your recommendation was Turbo Pascal. I took your advice, and when time allows, I am gradually learning Pascal.

Yet, Pascal has a deeper meaning in my life because of the man this language is named after, Blaise Pascal. Pascal, as you know, was the father of binary mathematics. And, with binary mathematics being the theoretical core of computer science itself, Pascal may logically be considered the father of computers (and Mr. Data). Simply stated, binary math bases its axioms on one essential theorem table: on or off, (0 or 1), or in linguistic terms: yes or no, true or false. A mathematical truth table determines the logical steps a processor must take to execute its calculations.

What Pascal devised on the mathematical blackboard he also applied to practical matters of everyday life—namely, the issue of binary truth as applied to the existence of God.[1] Thus he wrote "Pascal's Wager," which he used to intellectually challenge the society and culture of his day. This same wager applies to my life and yours. Please note the enclosed copy I made for you of Pascal's Wager.

In short, what Blaise is saying is that if Christianity is true, then we have everything to gain and nothing to lose by committing our lives to Christ. Even if Christianity is false, then one has gained at least one of the greatest moral teachings the world has known. But if Christianity is true, and we fail to embrace it, then we have lost everything and gained nothing. This is so because of all the world's "religious" leaders throughout history, only Christ made the claim that he was God and was the *only* way to heaven. Christ claimed to be the binary ON and only ON.

Steve, with all due respect and without trying to sound "sermonic," on October 12, 1974, I committed my life to Christ, and it has never been the same since. I was raised in the "church" and knew the story, but never met the main character personally until I made a volitional choice of asking Christ to live in me rather than me trying to live for myself. I used to think that Christianity was just one of the many options in the marketplace of religions.[2] I reasoned that since all religions ultimately believe in the same God, then a choice of a particular world religion or the creation of my own "personal religion" would suffice. I thought I could create my own, subjective commitment and perception of God and thus rule my own personal universe.

However, my commitment to Christ is based more on objective evidence than subjective feelings. In short, the compelling and overwhelming evidence for the reliability of the Bible as seen in the mathematical probabilities of prophecy and Christ's miracles, claims to deity, and His resurrection[4] as a yet unrefuted fact of history, not to mention other cogent reasons for the validity of Christianity, drew me to embrace its truth. Pizza, beer, and "religion" can give anyone a feeling. Christ gave me both intellectual *reasons* and subjective reality.

To become a Christian, one does not have to go to church. Christianity is not a series of hollow "dos and don'ts," but instead a personal relationship with God through Christ. In fact, Christianity is not a religion; it's a *relationship.*

When I committed my life to Christ, I did not see lightning, hear thunder, or hear birds and sweet music. I said a simple prayer and asked Christ to come into my life. I acknowledged that He was who He claimed to be (100 percent God and 100 percent man) who came to rescue me from my "bent" nature (as C. S. Lewis coined it in *The Space Trilogy*) by dying on the cross for my sins. I then started to read the book of John in the New Testament.

Steve, I don't have all the answers for why you have cancer or why God allowed your illness. If you still have the copy of my thesis I gave you, look at the last chapter that speaks of Lewis's experience with his wife dying of cancer. Lewis himself fought the same battle you are fighting. He lost the battle with cancer, but he won the battle with life. In fact, Christ said, "I am the Resurrection and the Life. He who believes in me will live, even though he dies" (John 11:25 NASB).

I will respect your decision if you choose not to comment on this letter, yet I am looking forward to discussing the contents if you so wish. I guess since we never directly discussed this topic, I wanted you to know what I would say to a person of your intellectual caliber facing the reality of your situation. Please understand, my intent is not to "preach religious doom and gloom." Forgive me if I come across that way. I just wish for you to have a treasure that will never cease. A treasure that will affect your life now and in the future, whatever that may entail.

The last page of Lewis's book *Mere Christianity* ends with one of the most powerful two paragraphs I have ever read. It is with these words I wish to close.

> Until you have given up yourself to Him you will not have a real self. But there must be a real giving up of the self. You must throw it away "blindly" so to speak. Christ will indeed give you a real personality: but you must not go to Him for the sake of that.

> As long as your own personality is what you are bothering about you are not going to Him at all. The very first step is to try to forget about the self altogether. Your real, new self (which is Christ's and also yours, and yours just because it is His) will not come as long as you are looking for it. It will come when you are looking for Him. Does that sound strange? The same principle holds, you know, for more everyday matters. Even in social life, you will never make a good impression on other people until thinking

about what sort of impression you are making. Even in literature and art, no man who bothers about originality will ever be original: whereas if you simply try to tell the truth (without caring two pence how often it has been told before) you will, nine times out of ten, become original without ever having noticed it. The principle runs through all life from top to bottom. Give up yourself, and you will find your real self. Lose your life and you will save it. Submit to death, death of your ambitions and favorite wishes every day and death of your whole body in the end: submit with every fiber of your being and you will find eternal life. Keep back nothing. Nothing that you have not given away will ever be really yours. Nothing in you that has not died will ever be raised from the dead. Look for yourself, and you will find in the long run only hatred, loneliness, despair, rage, ruin, and decay. But look for Christ and you will find Him, and with Him everything else thrown in.[5]

Sincerely your friend,

Stu

1. Since all the world's religions have conflicting views on identical and essential doctrines or issues, all of them cannot be right. Applying this same approach to religion, C. S. Lewis states that there is only one right answer to a math problem. And thus, Pascal, in a binary fashion, concluded that since only Christ among all the world's great religious leaders claimed to be the only way to God (John 14:6 [NASB], "I am the way, the truth, and the life, no one comes to the Father but through me"), then a wager must be made concerning the truth or falsity of the historic Christian worldview. Along this same vein, Lewis writes: "I am trying here to prevent anyone saying the really foolish thing that people often say about Him: I am ready to accept Jesus as a great moral teacher, but I don't accept His claim to be God. That is the one thing we must not say. A man who was merely a man and said the sort of things Jesus said would not be a great moral teacher. He would either be a lunatic—on a level with the man who says he is a poached egg—or else he would be the Devil of Hell. You must make your choice. Either this man was, and is, the Son of God: or else a madman or something worse. You can shut Him up for a fool, you can spit at Him and kill Him as a demon; or you can fall at His feet and call Him Lord and God. But let us not come with any patronizing nonsense about His being a great human teacher. He has not left that open to us. He did not intend to."

2. Christianity is not a religion (in the formal sense). Webster defines religion as man's attempt to get to God. In Christianity, God came to man. Finite man could not communicate with an infinite God through his own efforts. The infinite would have to pierce the finite, which was specifically done through the Bible and the person of Christ. Furthermore, Christ's greatest condemnations were against the religious establishment of His day. Christianity is not a religion, but a *relationship* with the living God through Christ.

3. There are three-hundred-plus prophesies or predictions regarding the life of Christ in the OT that are fulfilled in the New Testament. This consists of, at a minimum, an eight-hundred-year span between the Old Testament predictions and New Testament fulfillments. The probability of just eight of these prophecies being fulfilled is 1 in 100,000,000,000,000,000 as verified by the American Scientific Affiliation. The chance of forty-eight of these prophesies being fulfilled is 1 in 10 (to the 47th power). Furthermore, at least seventeen of all these prophecies were beyond the deliberate control of Jesus, thus the means of fulfilling them Himself were impossible (i.e., place and time of birth, manner of birth [Micah 5:2; Daniel 9:25; Genesis 49:10; Isaiah 7:14], His betrayal, manner of death [Psalm 22:16], people's reactions to His death [mocking, spitting, staring], and His piercing and burial). Hence, there is compelling evidence for precognitive knowledge behind the Bible that is beyond the ability of human writers. This fact alone, in addition to its reliability and accuracy, sets the Bible apart from any other religious book in existence.

4. The resurrection of Christ is one of the most well documented and authenticated facts of history. Numerous scholars have attempted to refute the resurrection with no success. The extrabiblical and biblical evidence is so strong that it would stand in a modern-day court of law. Such brute fact evidence for the resurrection is compelling evidence that Christ was indeed God in human flesh.

5. Lewis, C. S., *Mere Christianity* (New York: Macmillan, 1960).

Printed in the United States
by Baker & Taylor Publisher Services